HYDROGLYPHICS

REFLECTIONS ON THE SACRED

ALSO BY PHAEDRA GREENWOOD

Beside the Rio Hondo: A Memoir of Rural New Mexico

North with the Spring: An American Family Travels in Europe

Those Were the Days: Life and Love in the 1970s New Mexico (with Jim Levy)

Drinking From the Stream: Women's Prose & Poetry About Nature

ALSO BY SHAWN NEVINS

Subtraction: The Simple Math of Enlightenment

Images of Essence (with Bob Fergeson)

The Celibate Seeker: An Exploration of Celibacy as a Modern Spiritual Practice

The Resurrection of John Davis: A Screenplay

Adventures in Caving: Kentucky and Indiana

HYDROGLYPHICS

REFLECTIONS ON THE SACRED

Photography by Phaedra Greenwood

Poetry by Shawn Nevins

TAT Foundation Press
Hurdle Mills, NC

Published by TAT Foundation Press
Burlington Road
Hurdle Mills, North Carolina 27574
Tatfoundation.org

Main entry under title: Hydroglyphics: Reflections On The Sacred

1. Spirituality 2. Photography 3. Poetry

Library of Congress Control Number: 2019951318

ISBN: 978-0-9864457-5-0

Table of Contents

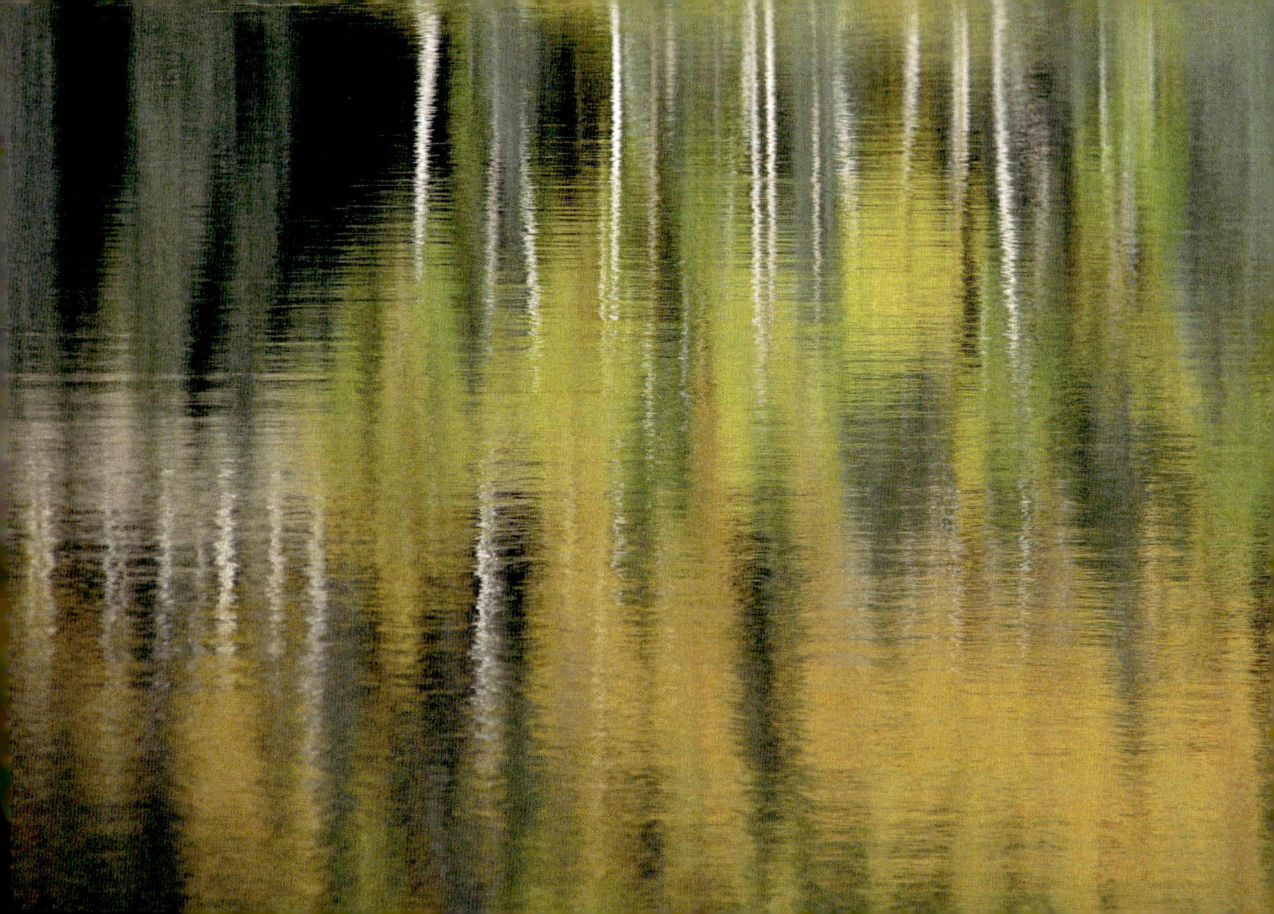

A Prelude

WHAT IS MOTION? What does the eye capture in a moment? Is the art of photography a slice, a glance that reveals infinities? A stopped watch holds us, poised over a chasm of revelation. Light, motion, photons, beam life from some unknown place. We press a button, put in motion a force which binds photons in place. What have we done?

Are we masters of time, or fools?

There is life or force or power that refuses to be bound. The truth is paradox: still but moving, frozen but alive. Much like the photographs in these pages.

Words, however, first dance. They are meant to move, meander, portray. As do the poems in this volume. Do words also bear stillness? Beneath their play is a vast silence. They, too, have another story to tell. Their presence also speaks of absence.

Words match, motion for motion, and share stillness with photographs.

How do we capture anything? A thought, an image, a curve of leaf margin in mid-day sun? We concoct, we dream, we remember, and if we're lucky on one auspicious and ordinary day, grace pours through and around our little selves and reveals.

A Note on Hydroglyphics

by Phaedra Greenwood

Growing up in Michigan, I often sought comfort in nature, perched on the end of a dock or sitting under a tree by the nearest river or lake. When I was twelve, I began to take solitary walks in the evening. The neighborhood was rural and it was considered safe for a girl child to wander around. Across the road lay a grassy field and beyond that, the woods. One late afternoon, just as I was about to leave the house, a storm blew in and drenched my hopes, but the rain let up before sunset. I banged the screen door behind me, jogged across the field and slipped into the woods. I followed the narrow footpaths, inhaling the heady scent of ozone, the wet fecund earth. In the cool green stillness the leaves were spattered with silver raindrops. Then the clouds thinned and the sun broke through the trees. Every trembling drop on every leaf shot forth spears of golden light.

I gasped in surprise at the sudden beauty, a jeweled fairyland. A wonderful sense of lightness stole over me. I lifted my head, alert to every flight and splash and quiver. My steps were sure and swift. I glided through the sanctuary of the forest like the deer, in a state of grace. Something in me knew that this luminous oneness with beauty was holy. All through my teens, wherever we moved, I returned again and again to the woods, the lakes and streams. Alone in light and shadow, I shed my anger and my fear, slipped off my shoes and waded into the secret that knew me.

It might seem strange that after high school I left wet, green Michigan and finally settled in the high mountain desert of Taos, New Mexico in a small adobe beside the Rio Hondo. I was soon immersed in a compelling life with a complex man I deeply loved, a houseful of pets and two active, healthy children. But I still needed time alone to stay centered.

In my stolen free time, I headed down to the Rio Hondo with my old Nikon. As I photographed the patterns of standing waves, I struggled to grasp the paradox of stillness within motion. Later I learned that standing waves are a standoff between two forces: the linear tug of gravity and the surface tension that shapes the droplets into perfect spheres.

My still photos revealed a hidden order in the seeming chaos of nature: swirls and curves, cross-currents and eddies that create unique counter-flows. Like snowflakes, no two eddies are exactly alike. Each manifests its own creative form. Golden honeycombs wavered on the bottom or flickered on the bank-side grasses in a pale caustic light. If I tossed a pebble into a quiet pool, ripples expanded in concentric circles called "quora," struck the banks and returned to center. On the hillside behind our house petroglyphs of quora, maybe a thousand years old, were carved onto the basalt rock faces. It was not just these elegant patterns that drew me back again and again. I sensed some inherent mystery. I would have to dive deeper.

Ten years ago when I bought my first digital video camera, I hurried down to the stream. The camera was capable of focusing on different levels: the inky reflections of branches outlined by a pale November sun; wave patterns where the stream narrowed; and the brown leaves drifting with the current below. I wondered about the string of round shadows that fled along the bottom. What was making them? I pressed the record button and followed them upward to discover spinning vortices on the surface.

I was off on a vigorous and sometimes euphoric exploration of the dynamics of moving water: crouching by a puddle in the pouring rain; slipping inside a waterfall with my umbrella; filming a golden mist rising from the frozen rio at five below zero, or capturing the flutters of moonlight at midnight along the banks of the acequias. The rhythmic moon-flutters my camera revealed whispered to me in a strangely familiar language I called "hydroglyphics." In winter glassy waves and spiderwebs of ice manifested along the banks of the acequia. Master Frost sketched flowery arabesques on top of the car, or pranced across our windows in starbursts and dendritic patterns.

I discovered books that became my touchstones of truth. Theodore Schwenk's *Sensitive Chaos* explains how the flow of water shapes the human body, the feathered network of arteries and veins, the spiraling in cochlea and retina. Even in the womb, water follows specific paths. Logarithmic spirals that spread from the center in regular curves are visible in seashells and sheep horns, in sunflower seeds and in the spiraling arms of the Milky Way. I understood that the universe is self-organized according to the laws of physics. I was not entertaining the idea of "intelligent design" nor was I longing for meaning. But floundering in the rip tide of human chaos, I hungered for fundamental order, beauty and wholeness. Searching for a perfect constant, I found myself in good company with Plato and his Form of beauty.

But the more I poke into perfect symmetry, the more it falls apart. According to Phillip Ball in *Patterns in Nature: Why the World Looks Like it Does*, symmetry is the fundamental scientific language of form, but ironically, shape and form arise from the breaking of perfect static symmetry.

So I bid farewell to Plato and drift into the peaceful Zen gardens of asymmetry where symmetrical forms may be used for meditation, but are not considered a fundamental part of nature because symmetry is transient. Thus the perfect symmetry of a Tibetan sand mandala is immediately swept away. In art balance can be achieved between asymmetrical elements by including the empty space. At the exit from the Zen garden, I contemplate the arrow of asymmetrical time that assumes we can travel in only one direction: forward toward entropy and equilibrium.

Equilibrium sounds peaceful, but it can be tricky.

Those who subscribe to the lovely Gaia theory of a self-regulated biosphere may think the world has always been in perfect balance, but what about the five previous mass extinctions? Balance is important if you're walking around in bilateral symmetry. But according to the Chinese Book of Wisdom, the *I Ching,* everything changes and changes. Breaks in symmetry may be caused by anything from an asteroid that wipes out the dinosaurs to a slight imperfection on the surface of a molecule. Peering at drawings of cubic layers of ice online, I'm falling through fractures in the surface called "stacking faults." And yet, from these "happy accidents" something new swims to the surface.

How about flow as a constant? Everything is pulsing waves—electromagnetic light waves, X-rays, sound waves. Or sometimes subatomic particles. And we don't know exactly where those particles are. They could be eaten by Schrodinger's cat. Electrons are whirling around in what is mostly space. I'm feeling woozy. So what are we really? And where do we come from? Dark matter? Antimatter? What gurus call "the teeming void?" My thoughts spiral around and around. What can I grab onto? I want to believe that there is something perfect within me, that manifests through me. Timeless and reflective. Like water.

What is water? I'm astonished to realize I don't really know. I escape for hours into complex models online—the drawing of a round red oxygen atom with two pale blue hydrogen atoms attached to its body by shared electrical charges called "covalent bonds." Other websites explain that everything we see takes specific form because of the collective behavior of its atoms. In steam, H^2O molecules drift apart. In water the molecules don't cluster but bounce and slide around each other. In ice they stick together with gulps of air between the molecules—that's why ice floats. Snowflakes are six-sided because ice molecules link up in hexagonal rings, the website says. I really want to see what that looks like. Hours later, I am up to my knees in four-sided pyramids called tetrahedrons.

I step outside for air. Breathe in; breathe out. That's oscillation. The blue halo around the Earth is in dynamic oscillation, too. Oscillation of temperature—the heating and cooling between the atmosphere and the oceans—is driven by the wind which is driven by the heat of the sun. In the global flow of the atmosphere, change is constant. Now I am looking for a still point in the center of oscillation. I suspect it has something to do with space-time.

Years ago I was lost at sea trying to understand Fritjof Capra's *The Tao of Physics*. I pick up the book again and open it at random to a chapter called "Space-Time." Capra defines it as "a living continuum in which space and time are integrated." According to the diagram, it's four-dimensional and interpenetrating. Those troublesome subatomic particles can manifest from nothing, then mysteriously disappear. They can glide backward or forward in time or sideways in space where everything is interconnected and exists simultaneously. Nothing is coming, nothing is going. Everything is nothing. The void is a womb both empty and full, the source of all life.

Now my hydroglyphics are laughing. The joke is on me. The constant I have been searching for is change.

Some people are not afraid of change. In fact, they seek it out. When Shawn Nevins first came to Arroyo Hondo for a visit, he brought his camera down to the Rio Hondo and set it on a rock to record the flow. Wow! I thought. We must be on the same wavelength.

Sitting on the couch after dinner, he tried to explain what he had experienced when he became enlightened–the dissolution of everything into the void. I got it later when I read his book, *Subtraction: The Simple Math of Enlightenment*, the lucid story of his long and often painful spiritual journey. I have not experienced the void. In my dreams I am teetering on the edge of a sheer cliff, terrified to let go. But I sense that my obsession with water will lead me to the great nothing.

Water is still my sacrament. I am fortunate to live in a place where traditional cultures feel that way, too. On the other side of Wheeler Peak—the source of the Rio Hondo—lies Blue Lake, the source of the Rio Pueblo that runs through historic Taos Pueblo. When I first arrived in Taos, a Pueblo woman told me, "Our lake is the most beautiful place in the world. That mountain is sacred. The water that comes from that mountain is sacred. I believe that when I die my spirit will return to Blue Lake."

I fell to musing about what makes Blue Lake sacred. Around the globe, some places are considered sacred because of the shape of the land or because something extraordinary has occurred there. Other places draw power from springs or natural beauty and are honored by rituals. Is Blue Lake sacred to Taos Pueblo simply because it's the source of the Rio Pueblo? Or is the lake made sacred by the annual pilgrimage of the whole tribe when they follow the stream back to its source?

Or… is that serene, pine-circled lake reflecting the blue sky sacred in and of itself?

If Blue Lake is sacred, why not William's Lake, the source of the Rio Hondo? Why not the Rio Hondo, too? The mountains I look up to every day are called the Sangre de Cristos, the Blood of Christ mountains, because they often turn crimson in the sunset. The Hispanos whose ancestors dug the intricate network of acequias and farmed the high mountain desert in Taos for over four hundred years called water the *sangre*, the lifeblood of the land. Driving through the Rio Grande Gorge one afternoon, I was struck by these Spanish words of wisdom scrawled on a smooth basalt boulder: *"No agua, no vida."* No water, no life. Can water be influenced by the power of our thoughts and feelings? Some believe it can.

Is all water sacred?

To me this feels powerful and true—water is sacred. Water is life.

"La vida es sagrada," Hispanos also say. Life is sacred. Buddhists believe that life is holy, in all its myriad forms.

So I honor the sacred flow on this planet, these brief glimpses of mystery and grace, and reflect them back to the still pool of collective mind. I hope that Shawn's poems will inspire us to leave our egos and fears behind and claim what we really are. Consciousness.

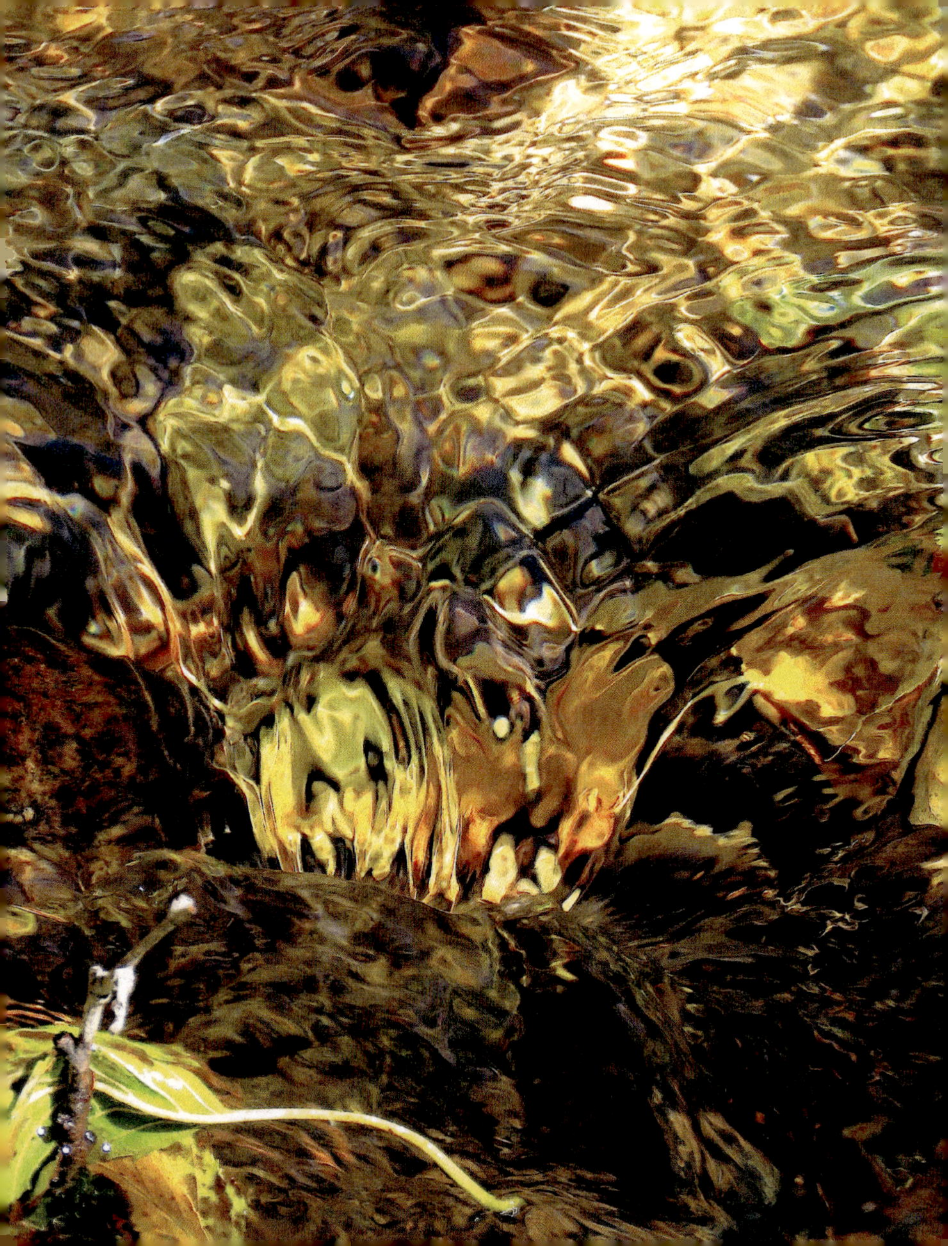

Go With The Flow

The scene: a stream
lit with the warm comfort of a harvest day,
topples over a smooth stone
and pours into itself.
We are that line,
where motion vanishes,
and the viewer's fiery heartbeat
pauses over an empty space within.

Painful and Glorious.

A hawk breathes the summer sky in which it soars,
as myriad expressions of being,
explode in infinite directions.
Wild wind and cries of joy wrap each dive into life.
All the while, below,
Love shakes and shimmers upon the water
even as the stream murmurs of loss
and cradles each drop of itself in stillness.

"O' paradox, where shall we find rest?"
Your emerald eyes ask of mine.
Place your hand with me.
Vision leads us,
like the pull of a tree toppling in empty space,
going with the flow,
cascading into our Real Self.

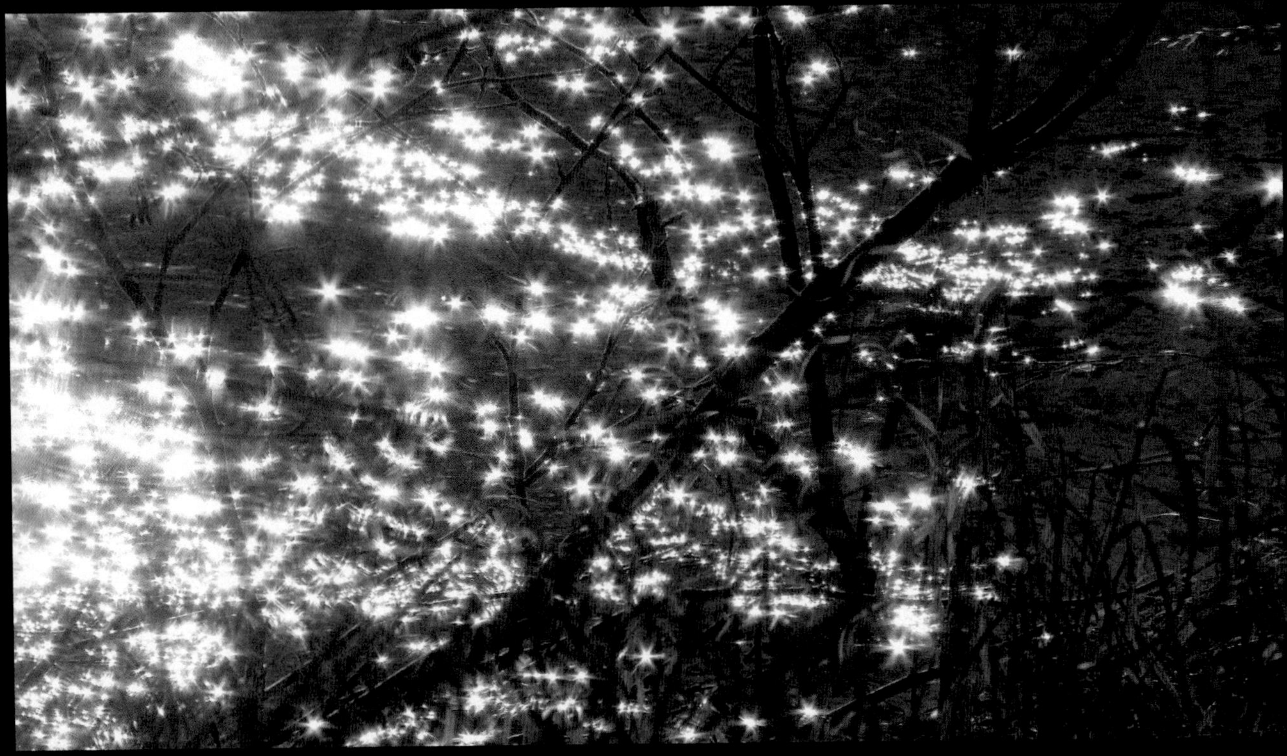

Everywhere Electric

A calm wind scales the wall of my self
stealthily.
A slow chill tightens restful arms
closing around the body.
Hair rises, whispering on the nape of the neck.

Everywhere electric,
everywhere more and more.

Every leaf vein, every knot of driftwood,
every flower draped over rock edge,
every fallen leaf, seed, bark, and insect.
Every moment picture is crying,
whispering, shouting, intoning
that it exists and that it does not.
It is up to you
to kiss and never hold again this life.

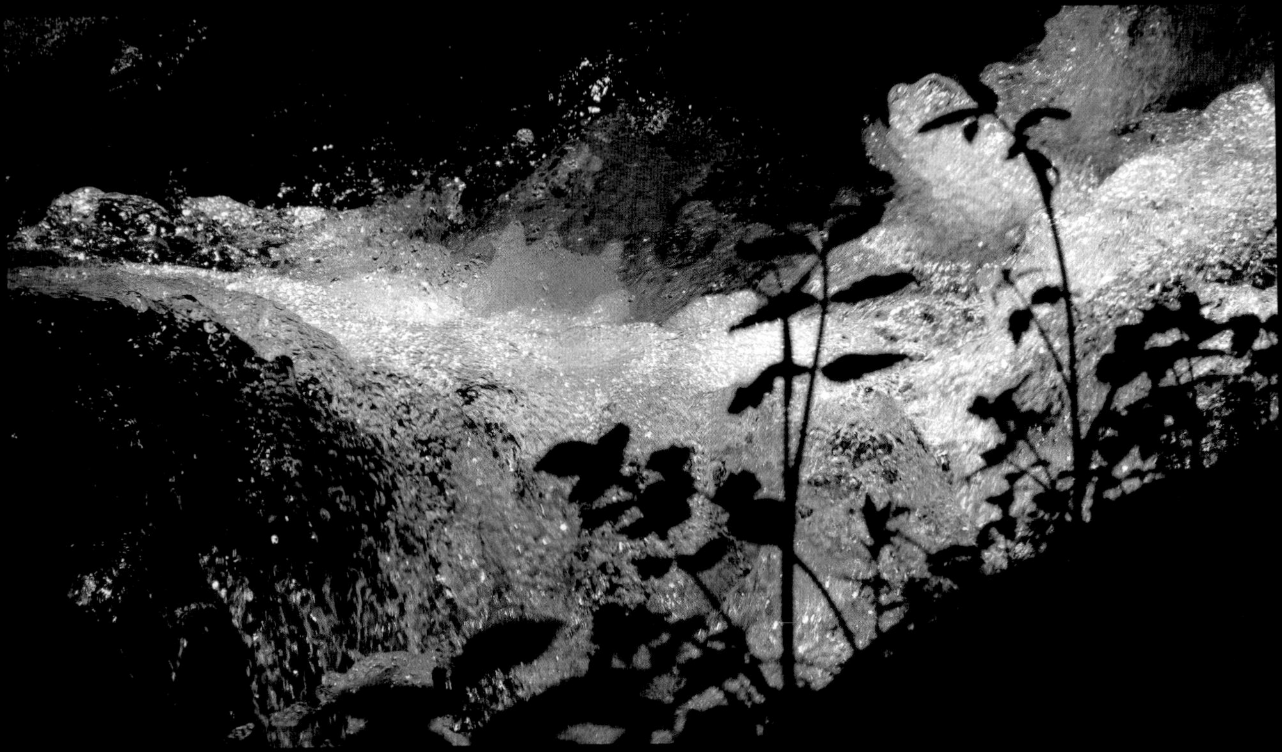

Brook Splashes

Where is meaning
when the sweep of time commingles
blood and bone, leaf and stone?
There is only a plunging forward,
a spray of individuality shimmering in the sun,
a million billion articulations of love.
And a twisted word called "meaning"
that hangs in space
demanding an answer,
while below, and around, and above
all borders blend into one.

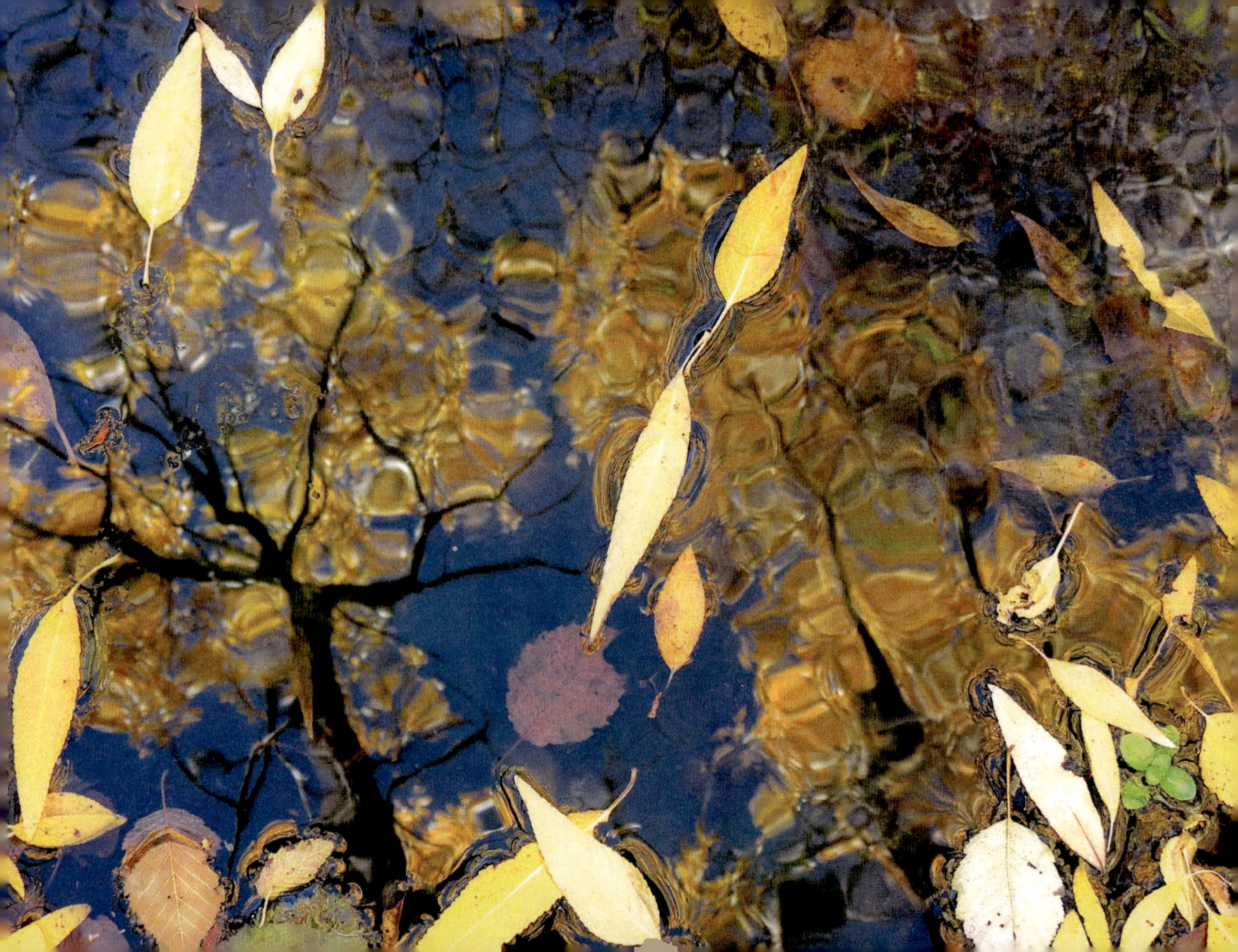

Cottonwood Reflections

A tree sees itself
in still waters
and bends towards that reflection,
breaking through the surface of things.

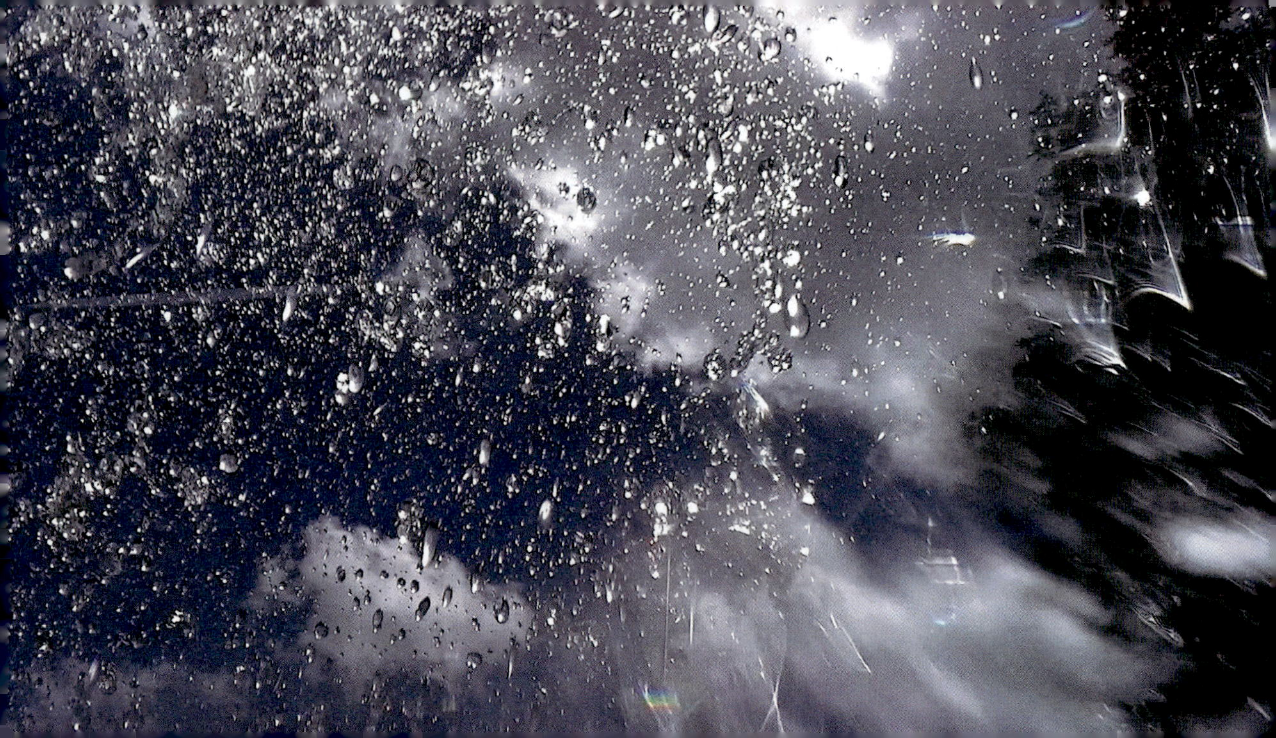

INSIDE A WATERFALL

If I could see *you*,
without the drape and fall of preconception,
without my drop of self
splattering its contents in every corner.

If I could see *you*,
without pleading,
without needing the universe to answer
with something other than another question
or suggestion of eternity.

If I could see *you*,
in the obvious, painful and beautiful
transience of phases,
and the roaring silence that sings praises.

If I could see *you*,
if that happened,
inside a waterfall,
it might look like *this*.

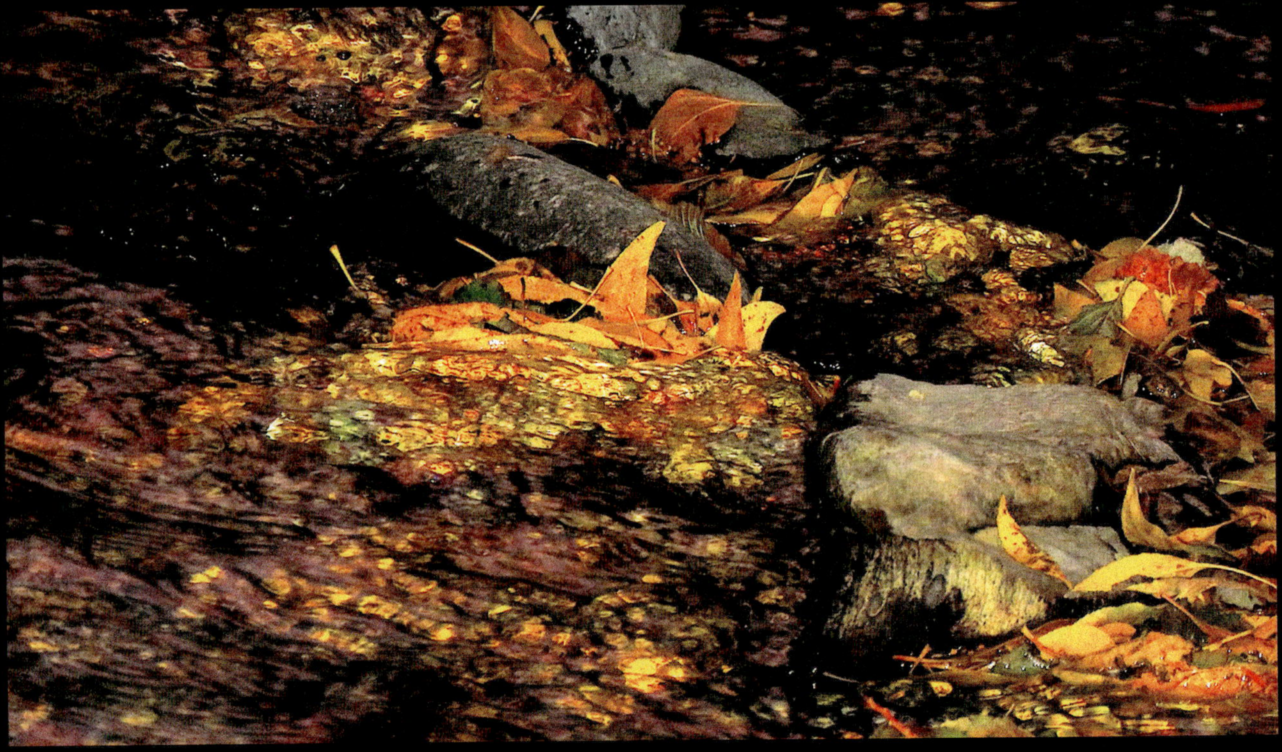

Hidden Treasure

I wait for you
at the meeting place,
where riveted attention holds thought,
and self begins to slip away.

I am there,
where you and I become welcoming waters—
pure, dark, deep, and full.
Where all is lost
and all is found
in this ever deep, ever still home.

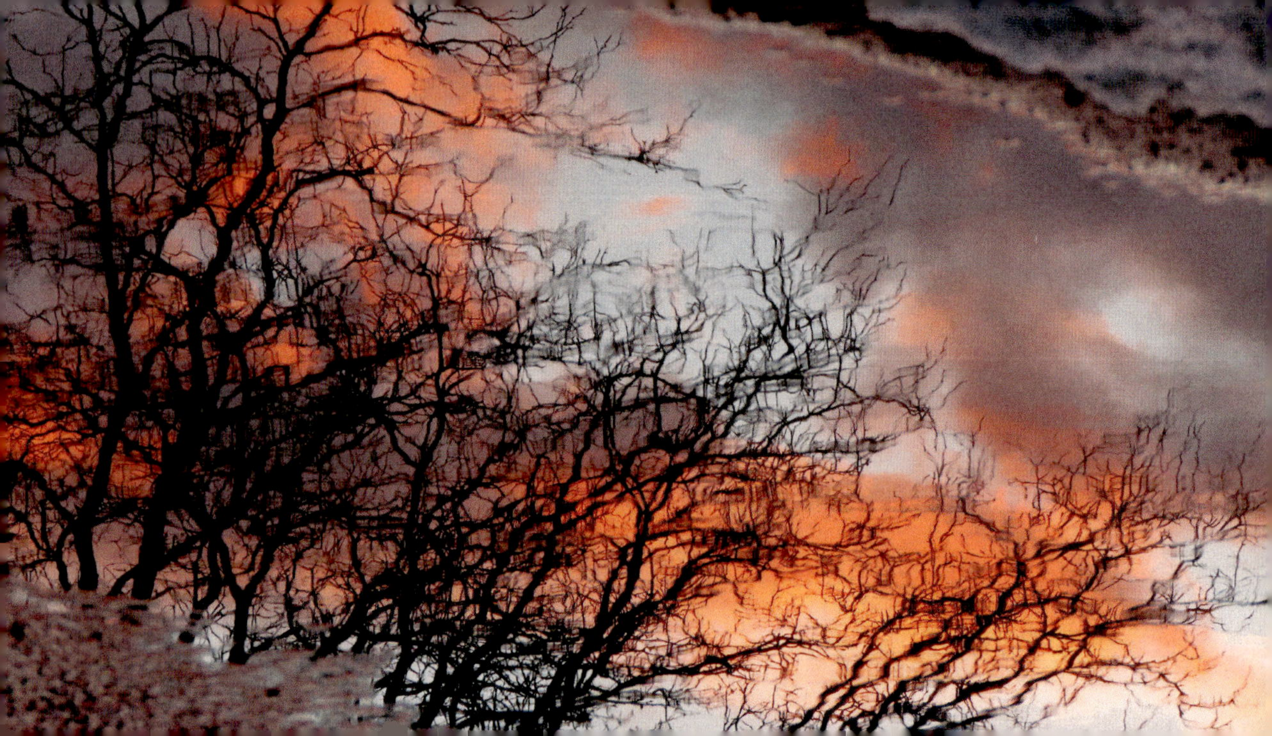

A Sunset Puddle

As she walks, the wind blows,
or does the wind move her?
Parting the grass made crisp by fall
her every step is recorded in time.
Time is the seasons of grass,
the spinning of planets,
the motion of infinite particles.
She is filled with love of particles,
with love of self,
even of the grass that, in time, will cover
her steps of existence.

She and I and you
blend into one long chain of events,
like clouds
bound by law to return to the sea.

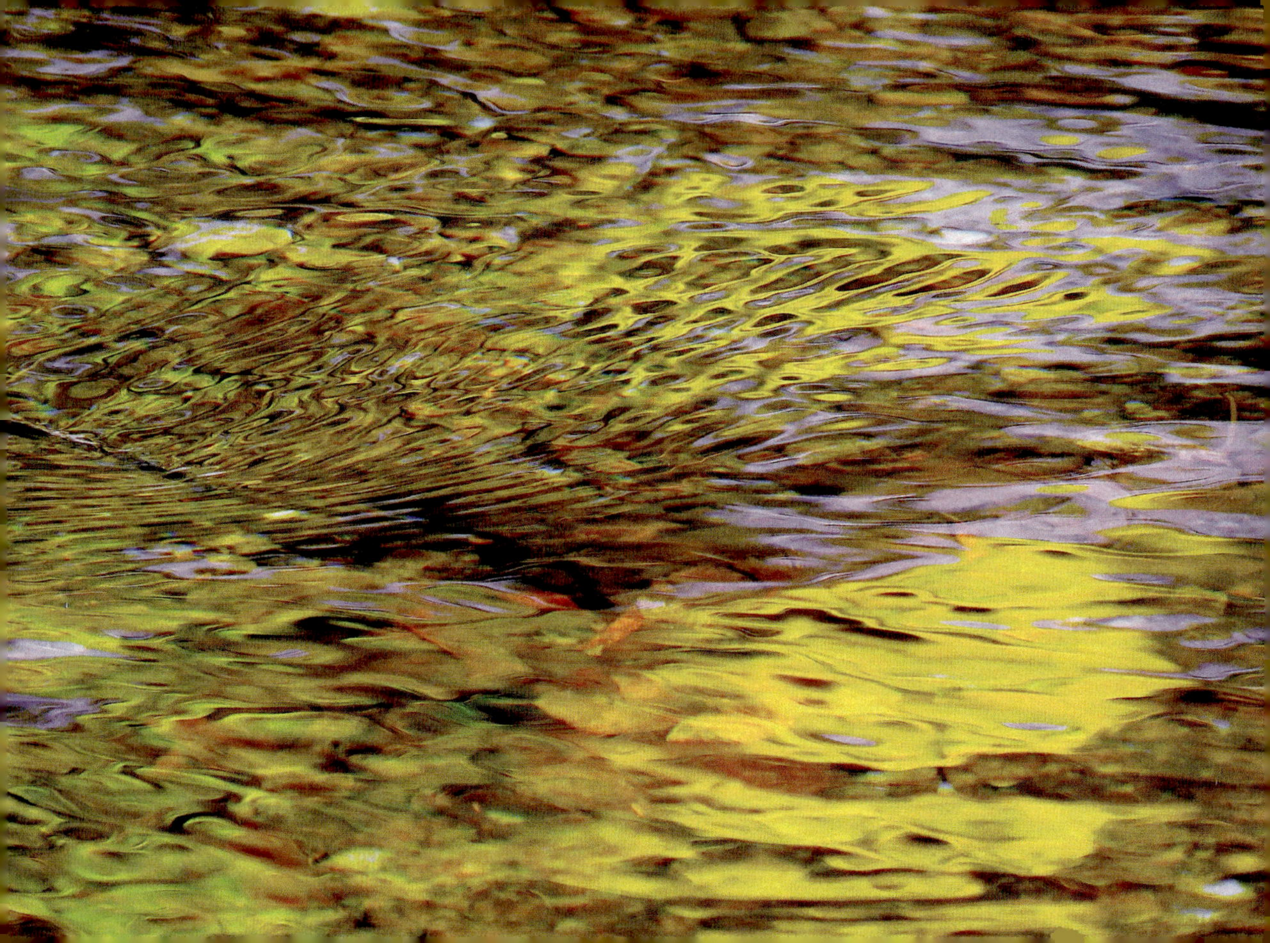

Aspen Reflections

I prefer to draw straight lines and labels
that say "This is me" and "That is you,"
but the more I look inside for a shore
on which to anchor my scheme
the more the particulars recede –
becoming suggestions of solidity
and rumors of the real.

What I find instead?
You and I are a child's set of paints
swirled together by the gravity of its joy.

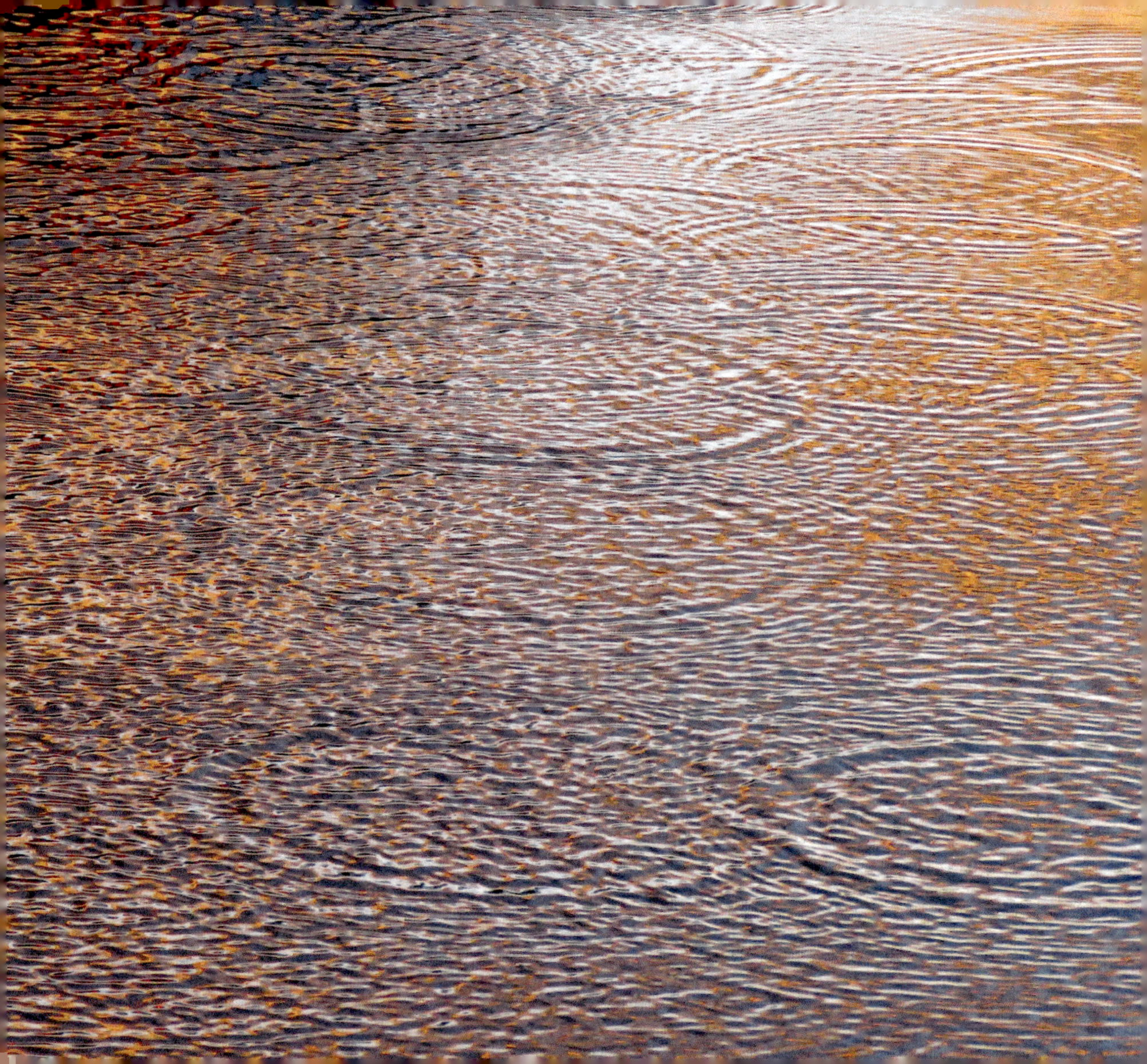

Circles

Between apogee and perigee,
Between the reach and the pull
Water swirls in all directions.
Right now, I can be…
Anything.
Walking a fine line of wetness
Between the poles of coming and going
I open in all directions.

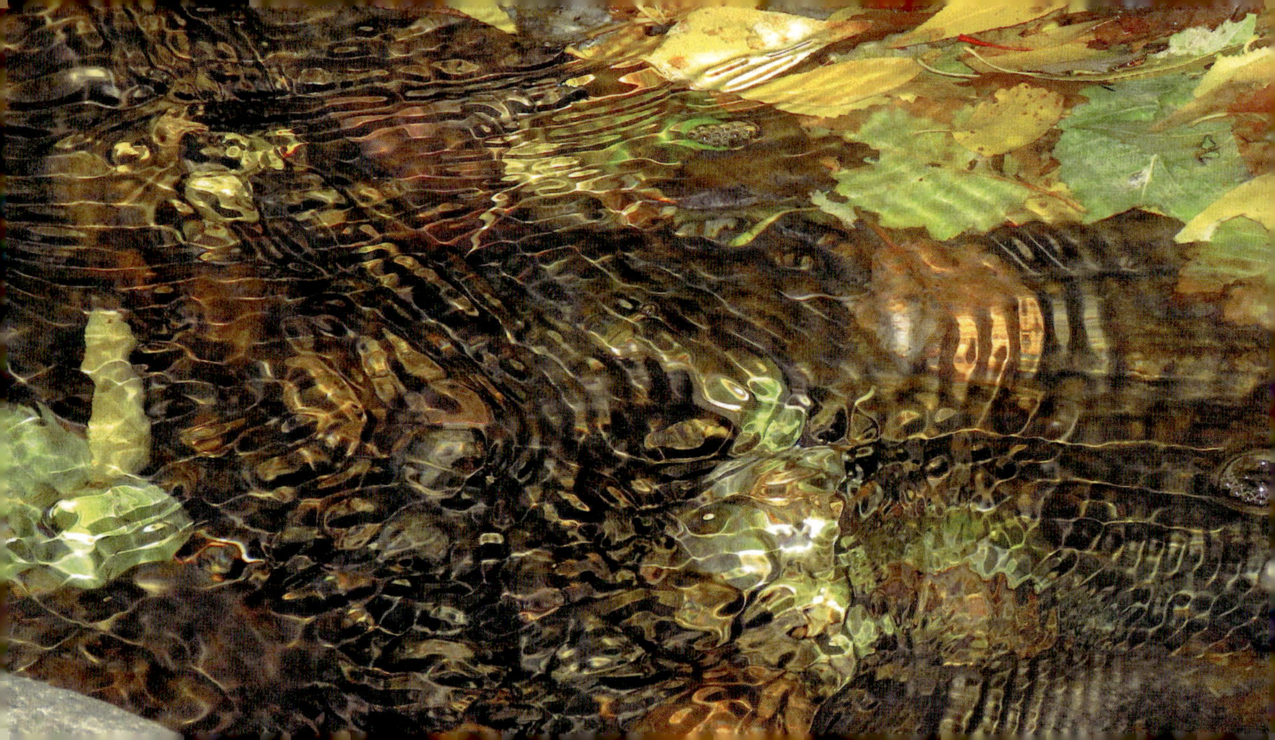

Fall Harvest

The clasp of strong hands, sweat of labor,
and elegance of exertion
—brotherhood of life—
bonded by the beauty of existence
and the sweetness of our struggle.

From molecule to miracle, everything moves
in a perfect pattern,
each piece as complete as the whole.

The air is thick with living;
even death pulses with possibility.
We are carried upon the water.

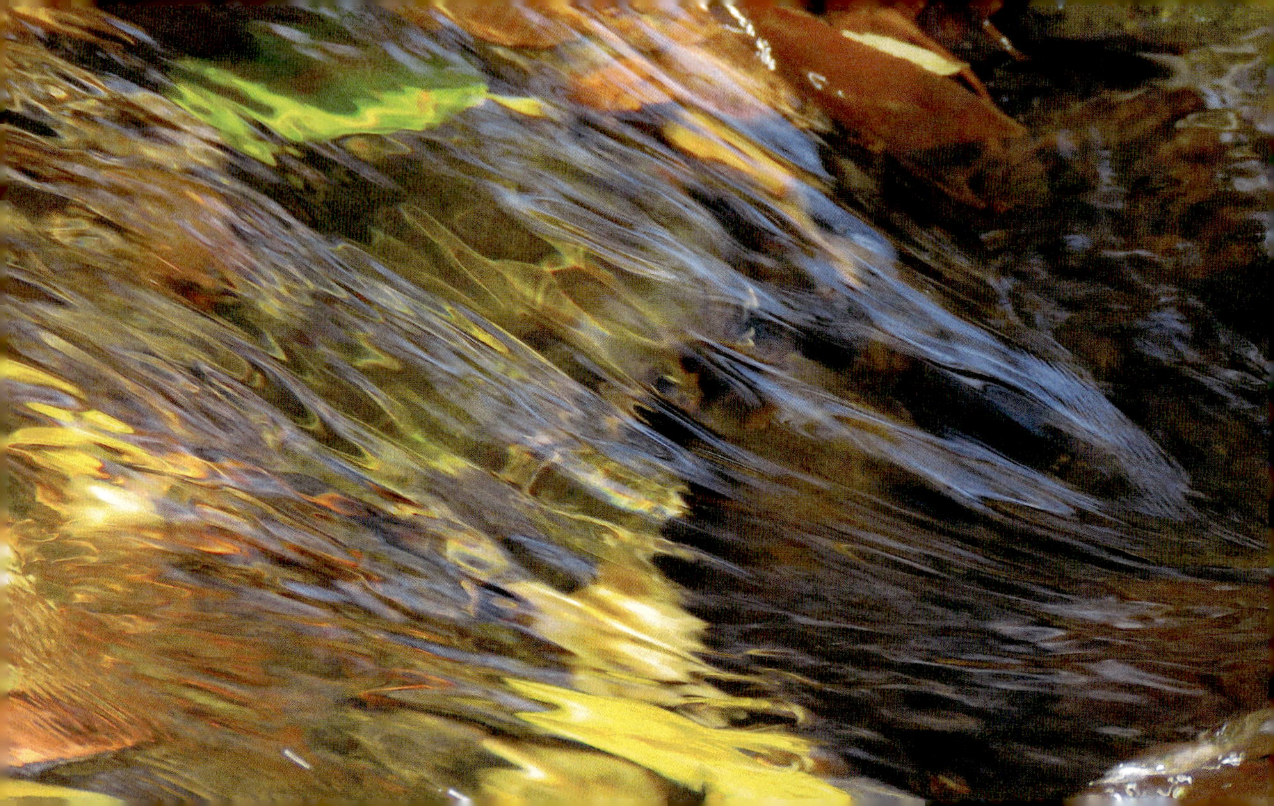

Water: Autumn

From a distance:
sweeping, soundless movements,
the grace of living showing itself,
pouring over all our objections
of *not enough, more* and *less,*
too far and *too late.*

The sun on a southward hill
washes darkness from the forest
and sweeps me downstream
deep within my self.

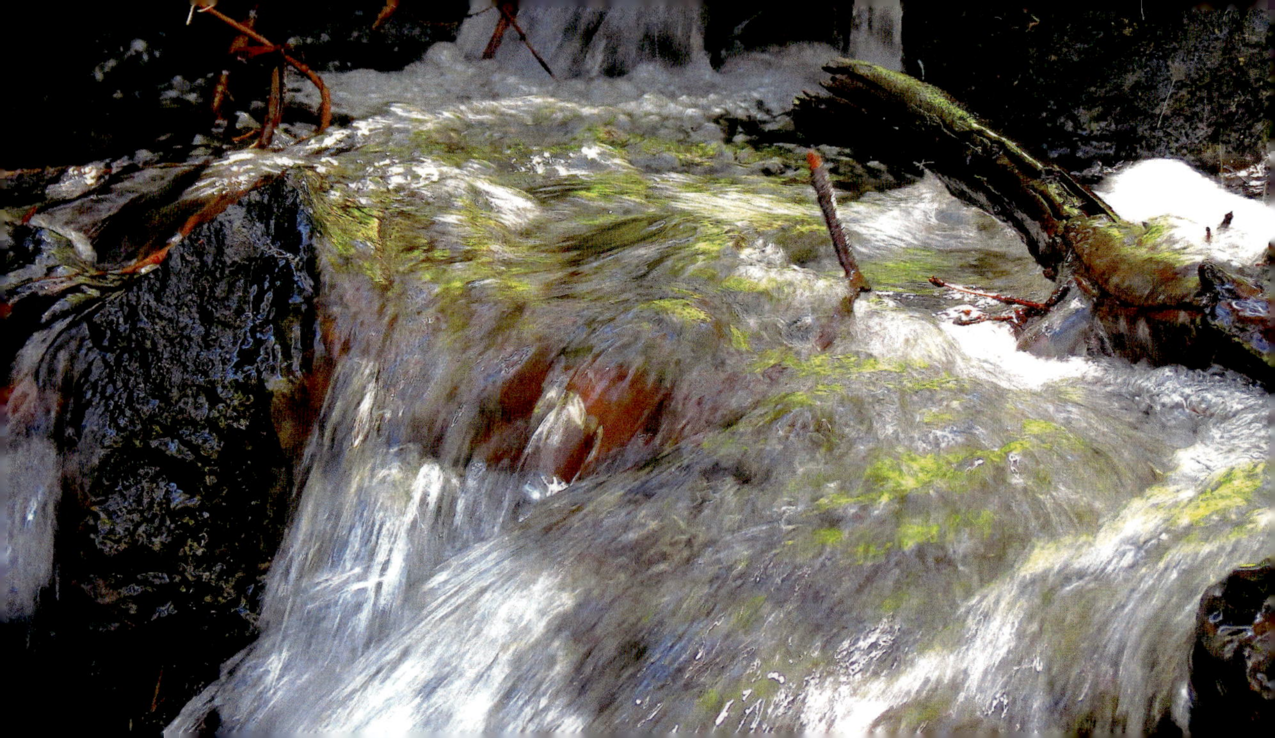

Mountain Stream

I've lost the sense of you in this noise;
the mad, rambling song of stone and leaf
under siege of change.
I've lost the sight of you in these rippling facets;
the camouflaging color of the eye's distraction
under seduction of form.
What was I looking for and why?

It's no matter.
There is nothing to be found
outside of this water dancing,
outside of the liquid jewel my heart becomes.

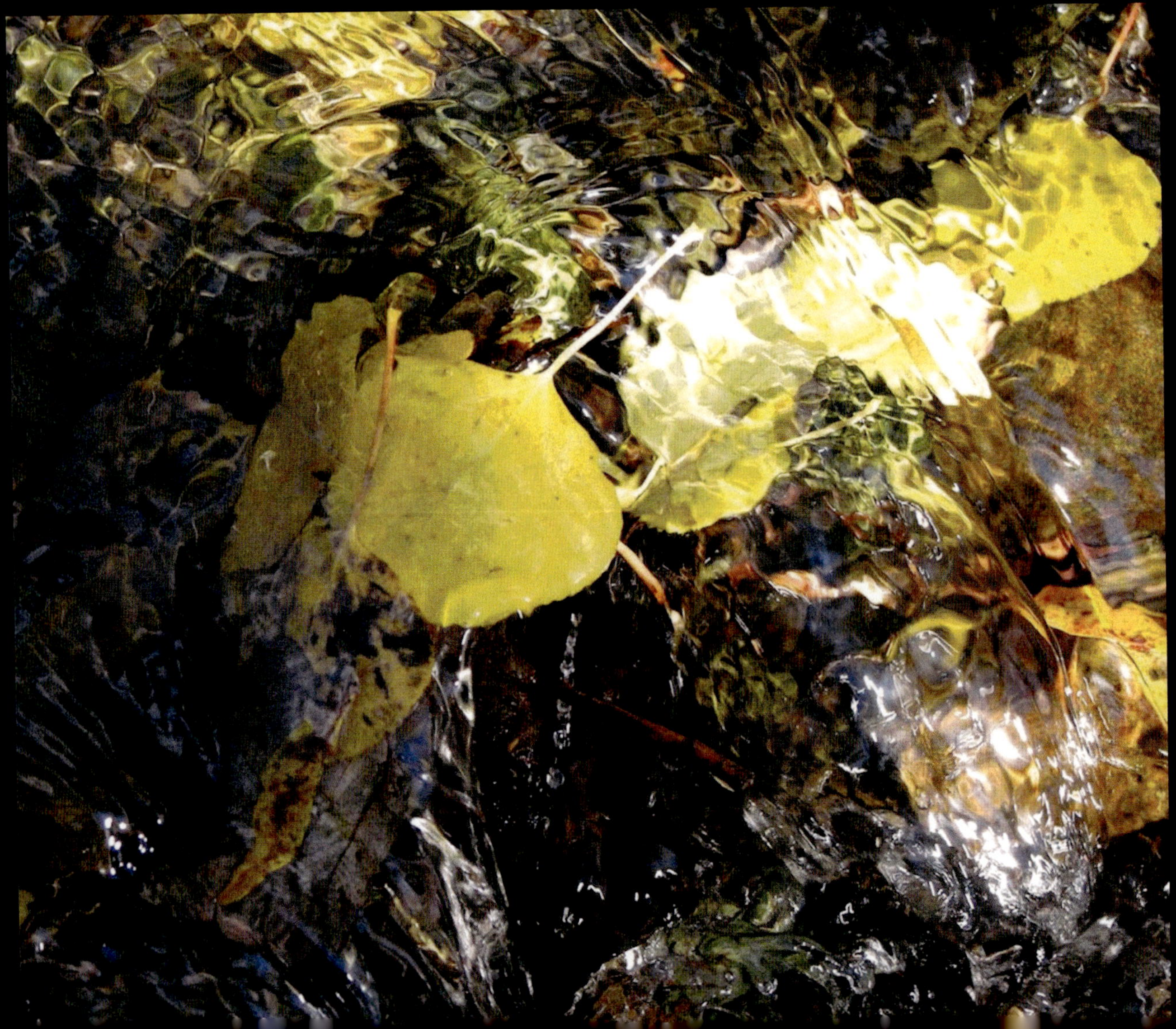

Aspen Leaves In Stream

I'm falling off the edge
of the edge.
The point,
the moment,
water breaks free of its bond to itself.

I catch myself catching myself
in the act of being conscious;
in the act of being aware, awake,
alive.

Like an eye, staring down a deep, swirling hole,
following the drops of moments,
finding itself at the very bottom.
Just heartbeats of feeling
and a beautiful nothingness between.

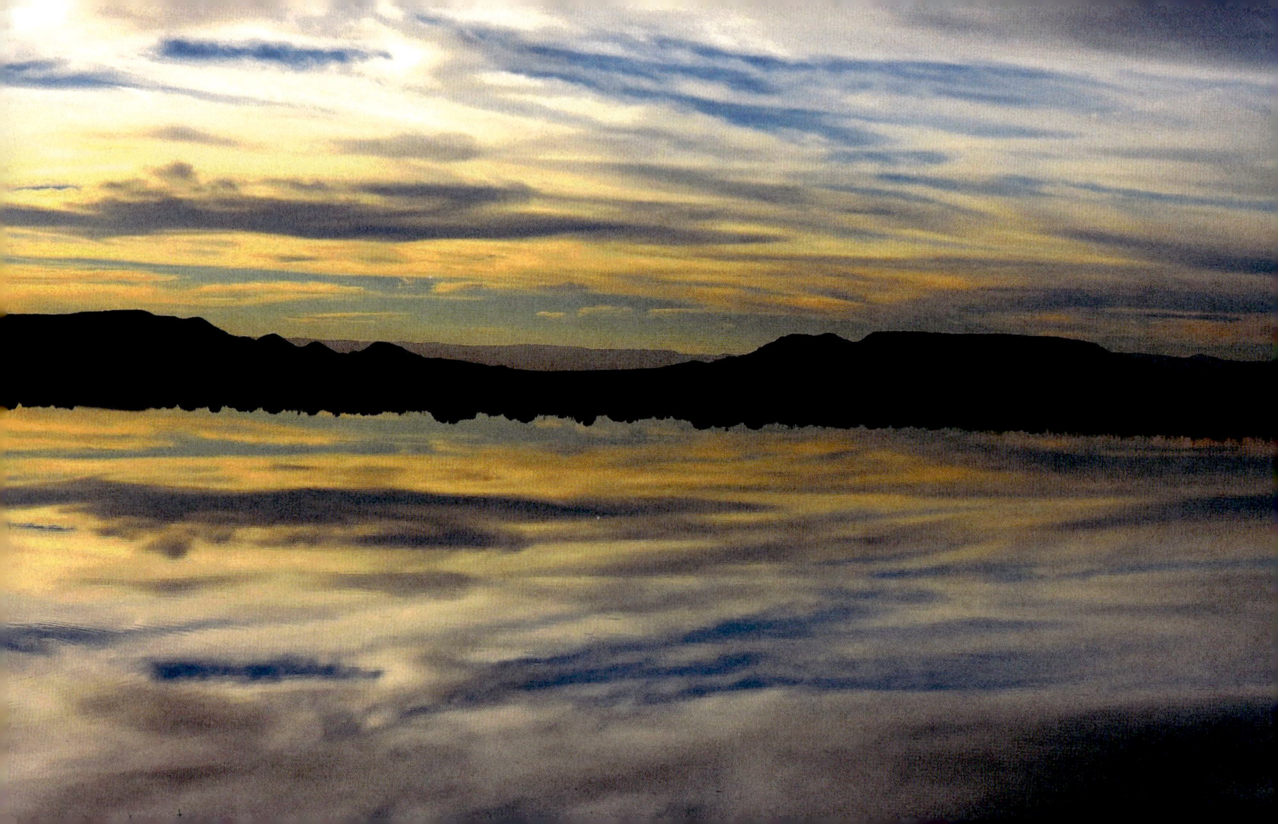

Sky Lake

Floating in early morning denial
Of the impending rise of my self
I hear birdsong begin and end,
The shake of a branch departed
The scuffling of feet on pavement,
The rise and fall of an engine's toil.
These sounds feign time
Pretending to wake the sun
Like the will of some hidden god.
I will never rise from this bed
For I am always, in every moment, dying.
I will never rise from this dream
And the pieces will fall away
Bird, song, sun, breath, darkness, silence
Becoming indistinguishable
In their unbecoming.
Love always tilts toward death.
Furling, shriveling.
Awakening is the first moment
After which there is no other moment
But this.

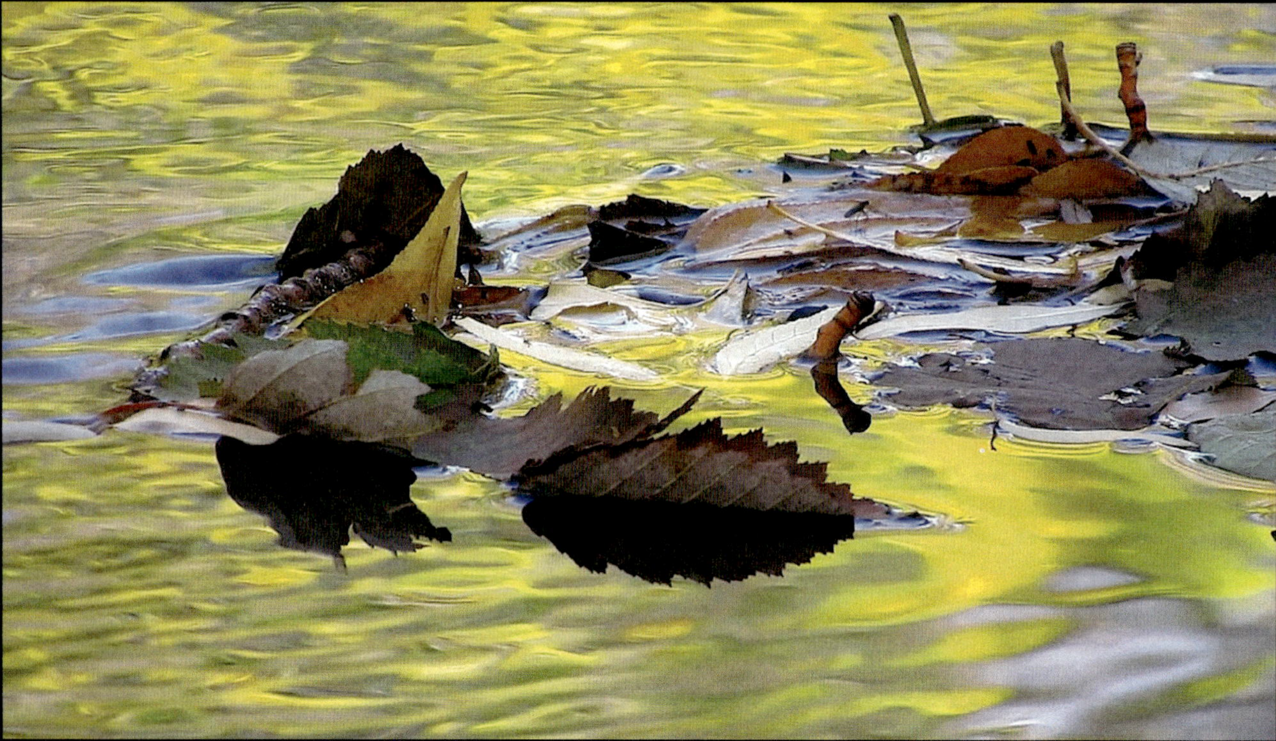

Leaf Raft

Life is a series of misleading loves
that eventually fall
like leaves pulled from autumn trees,
floating in patterns
away from you.

Your claim to a season
ends,
passes on,
becomes more
than any pattern or purpose
ever conceived.

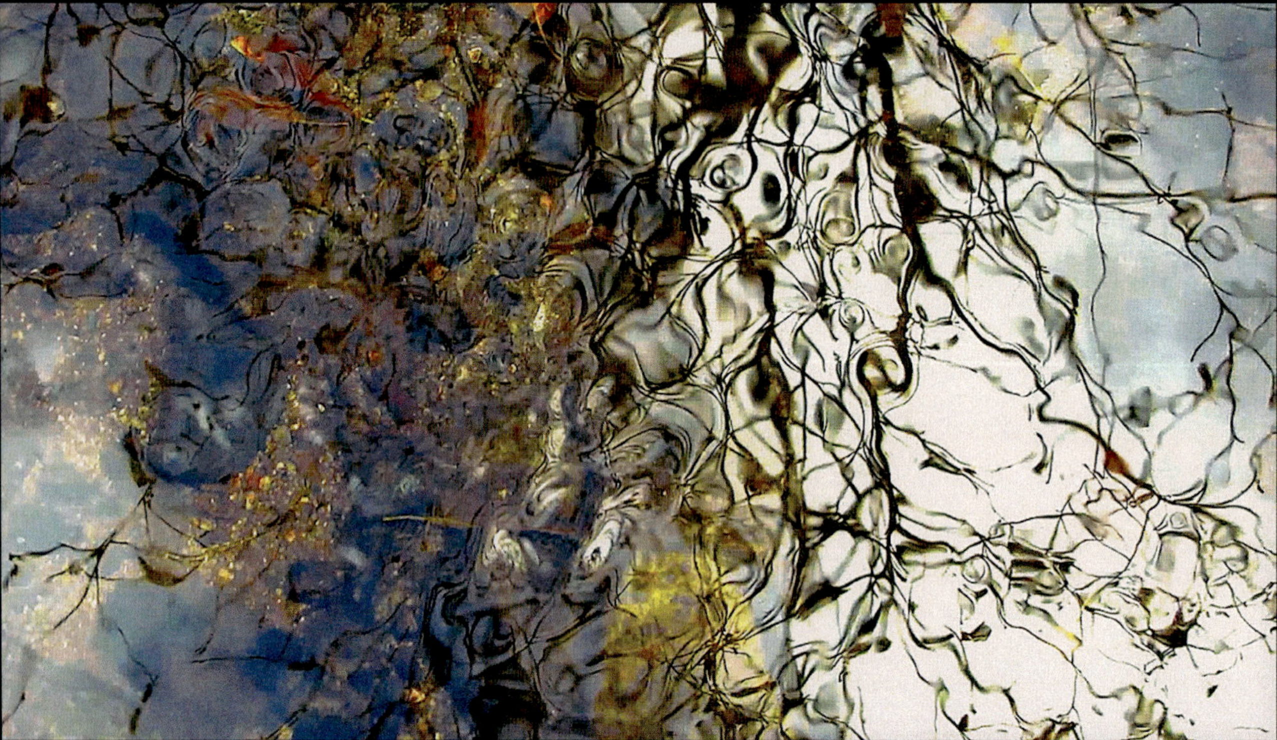

Cloud Cover

Life is white clouds painted on a blue sky.
A breeze hinting of coolness.
The sun warming your skin.
The understanding that every motion is proper;
every action is just.
That God is grace in motion.

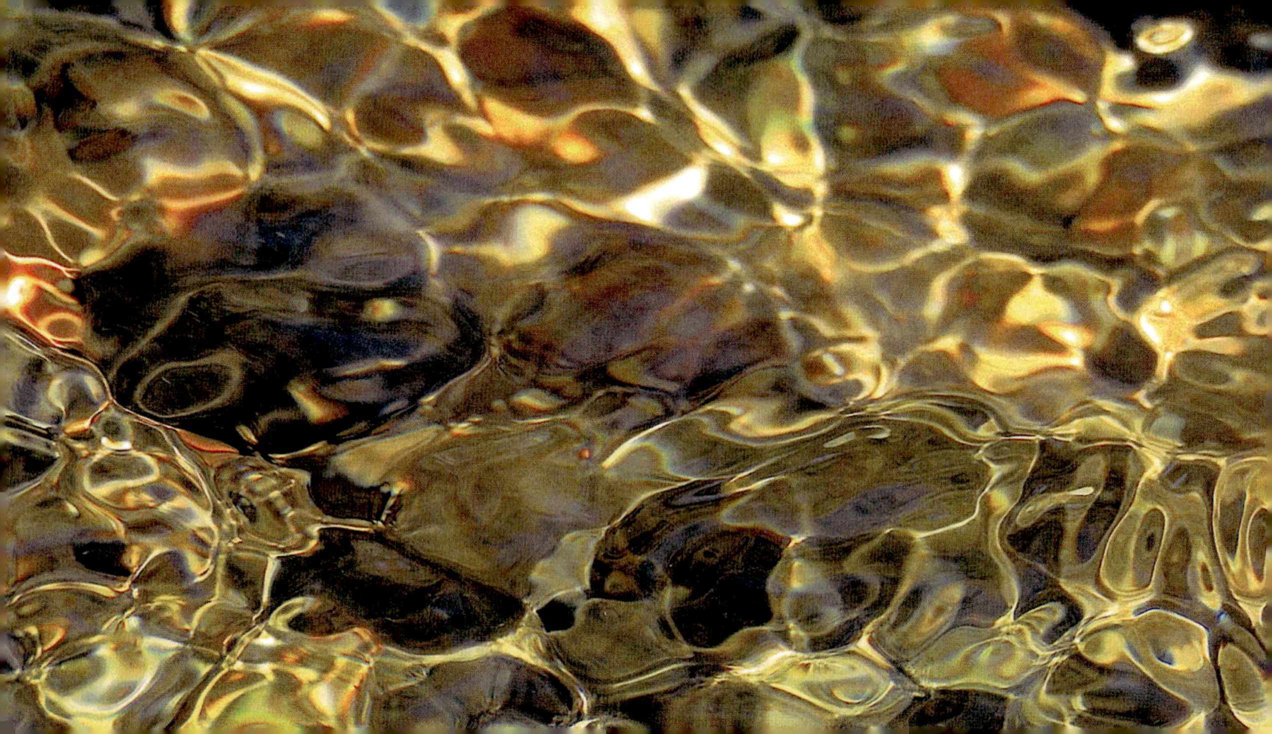

Water Over Pebbles

At sunrise,
a lambent column of light
extends across the water
calling you to meet it
—Out There—
where the universe pauses
and truth is revealed.

Sunlight fractures
into myriad reflected creations
each sparkling for a moment—
on and off, on and off ....

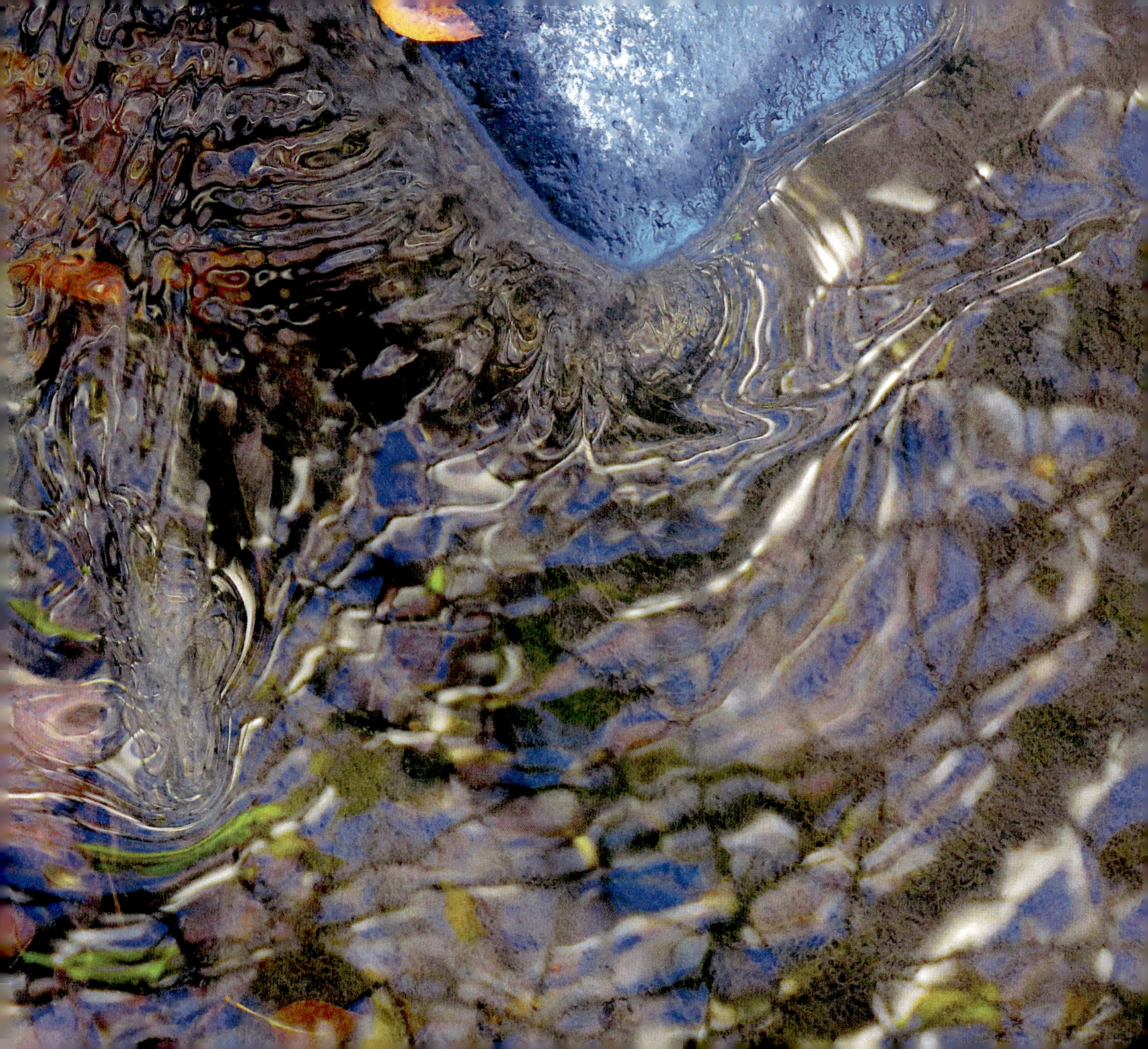

Blue Stone

Thought stretches out, looking for a reflection,
an affirmation, a substantiation,
but the swirl at the margin of sensation
sweeps me up like a breath billowing forth,
both with and without an edge of existence.

This trailing off of the seeming solid,
this path outward and back into the self,
this sapphire blue arising all around me,
takes me in my own arms like an impossible lover.
Familiar in a way I once knew,
like a word ripe for this moment, forgotten.

It's just a blue stone, but I won't come to this place again,
yet I will walk with you, everywhere, in all things.

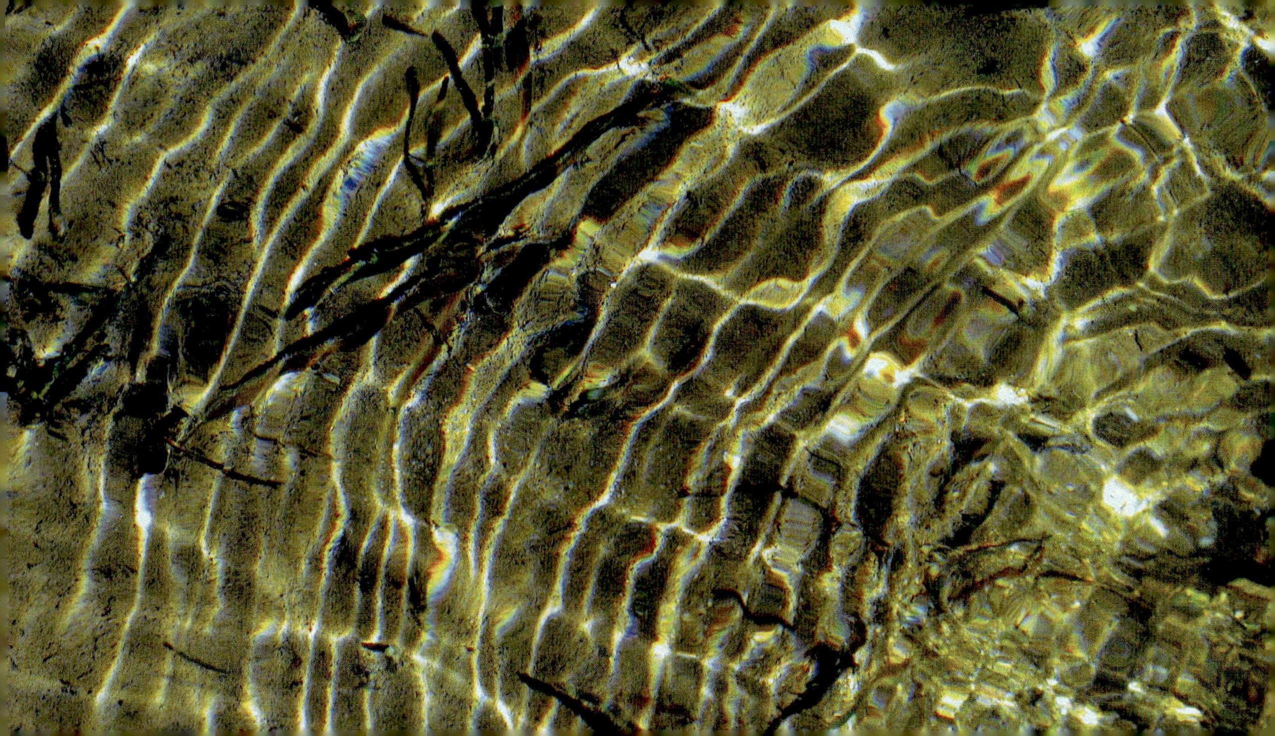

Resonation

Sorrow, joy, dreams a few
the passing wave and the mountain view,
the rippled sand and thought that cries,
the brazen brand of self's own lies,
called to home, called to now.

The grasp of hand, the bend of bow,
that fought for life and lived to show,
called to home, called to now.

Yes and no; leap and fall;
the stars themselves and the land that calls,
called to home, called to now.

The tear that winds through time and space,
the smile of one who seeks their place,
this flow of time and flick of life,
this end of rhyme and end of strife,
called to home, called to now.

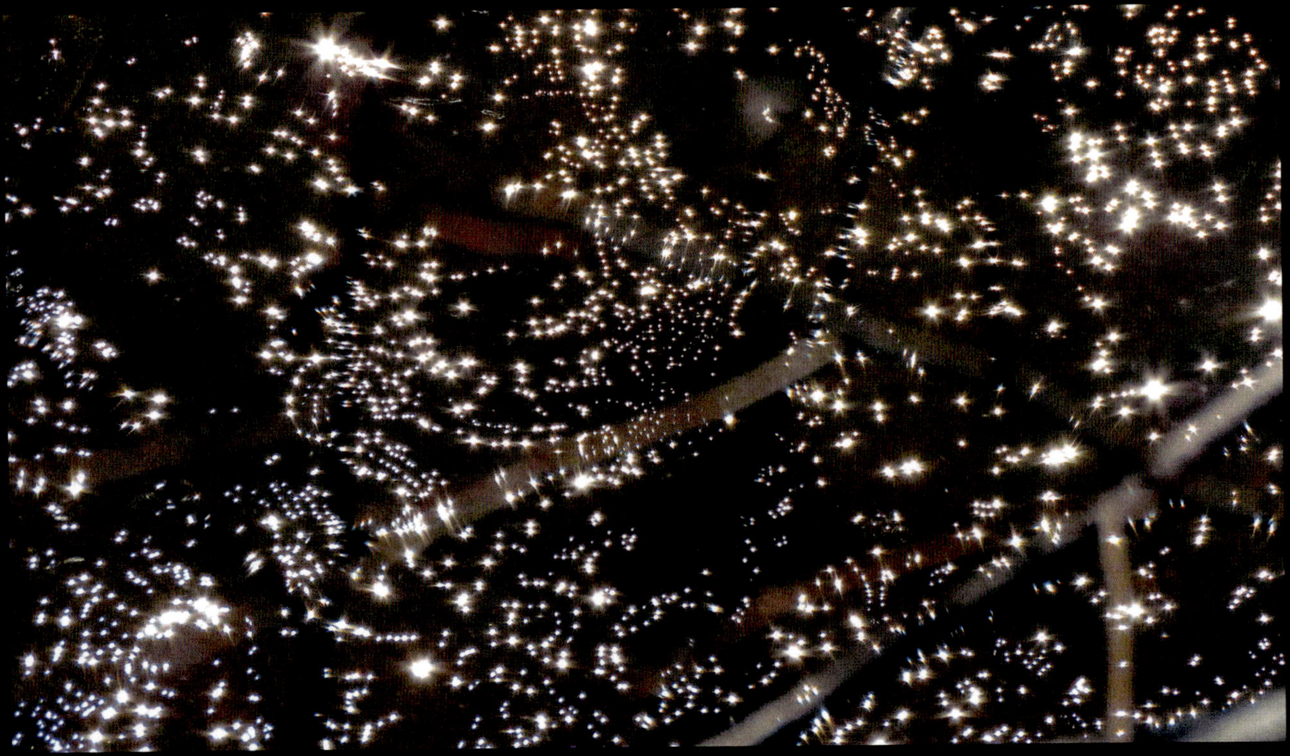

Hydroglyphics Of Light

A crow glides in silently:
like a suspicion of truth,
like the momentary fall of winter light
through a blind.
Illuminating a familiar room
—a life—
in mystery,
in significance.

The crow rises,
cawing, escaping our attention,
as clouds obscure the vision.
Still....
Still there lingers
the transparency of light, sound, and self
in which every moment shines.

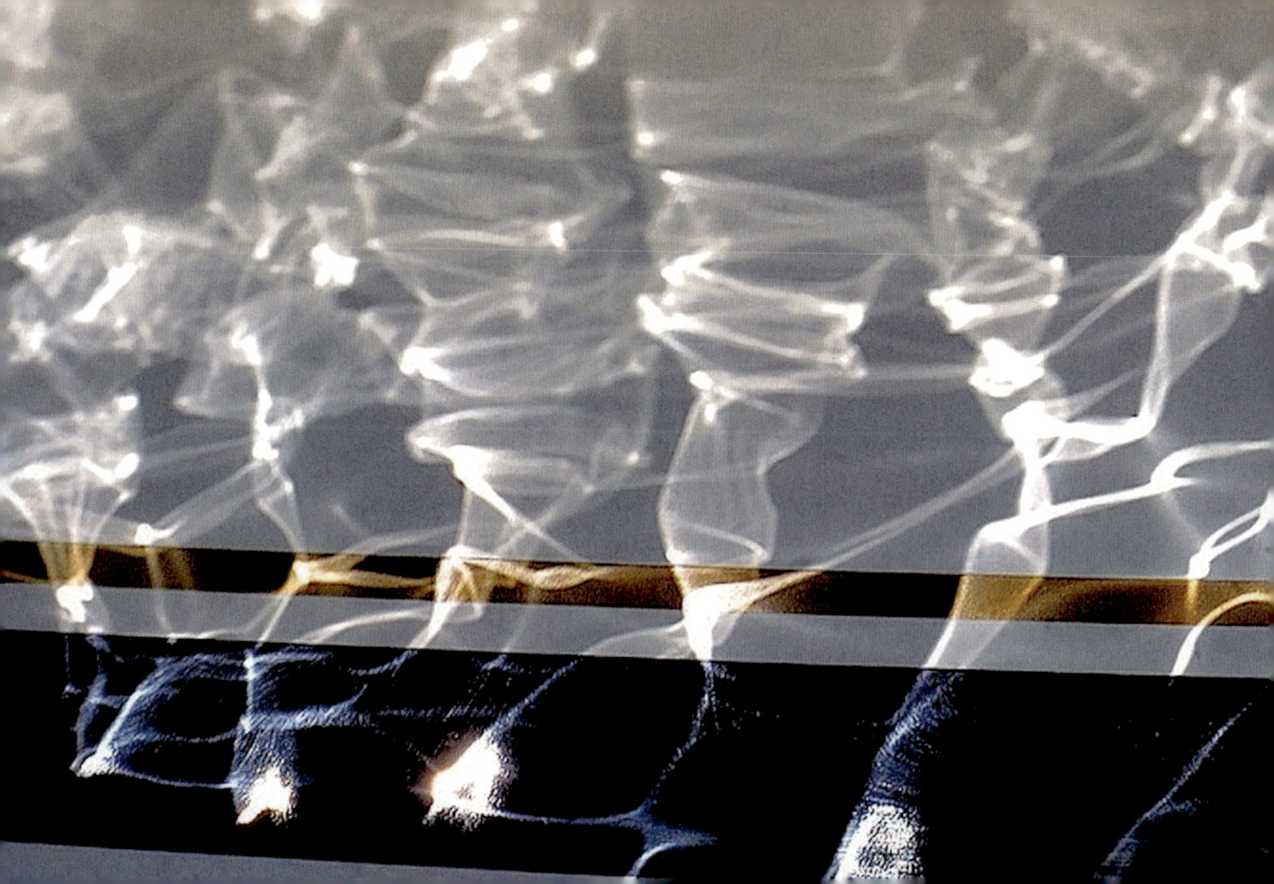

DANCING SHIP

A photon's long journey from the sun
is equal parts effort and grace,
which is not that hard to imagine,
for a creature both here and not here,
particle and wave.

I imagine the meeting of these qualities
like the scalloped turns
of pure reflection in this photo,
and like the curve of meaning
as these words form in your mind.

I imagine the bond of effort and grace,
being-ness and non-being-ness,
looks and sounds like this holy moment,
creeping up the back of your spine,
unrolling before your vision,
inhabiting the intersection of turn within turn.

When we cross paths like this,
on our long journey from the Sun,
there's no more imagining.

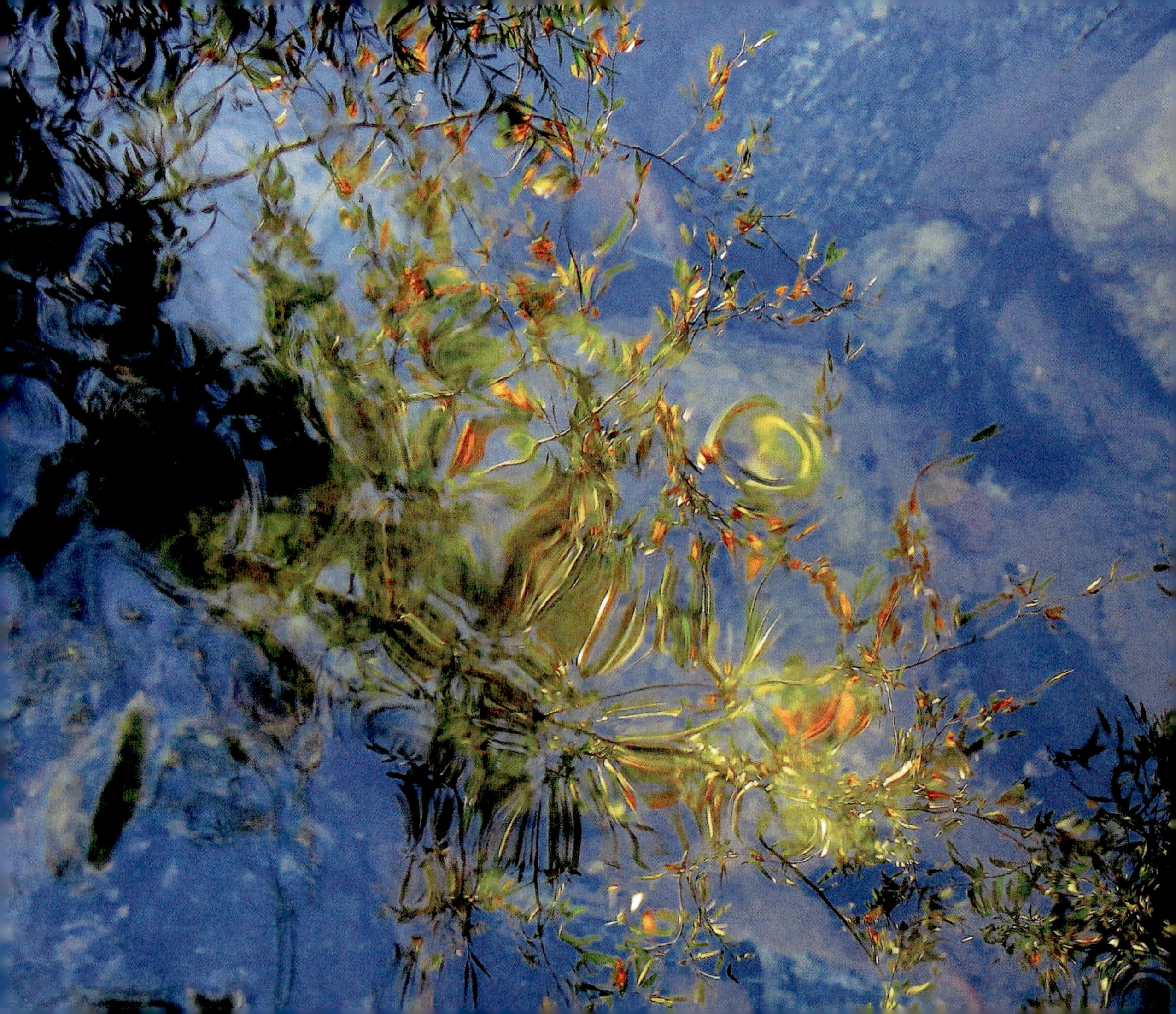

Sesame Vortex

Interspersed among the moments of your life
are pauses:
sun glinting off water,
a look of loss,
a bare branch against the sky,
a cool evening,
a breeze in the leaves.

I want to stop your mind
with the feeling of love that is leaving,
with a deep look inside,
with an unblinking opening
to the empty light within you,
with these lonely words,
with pauses.

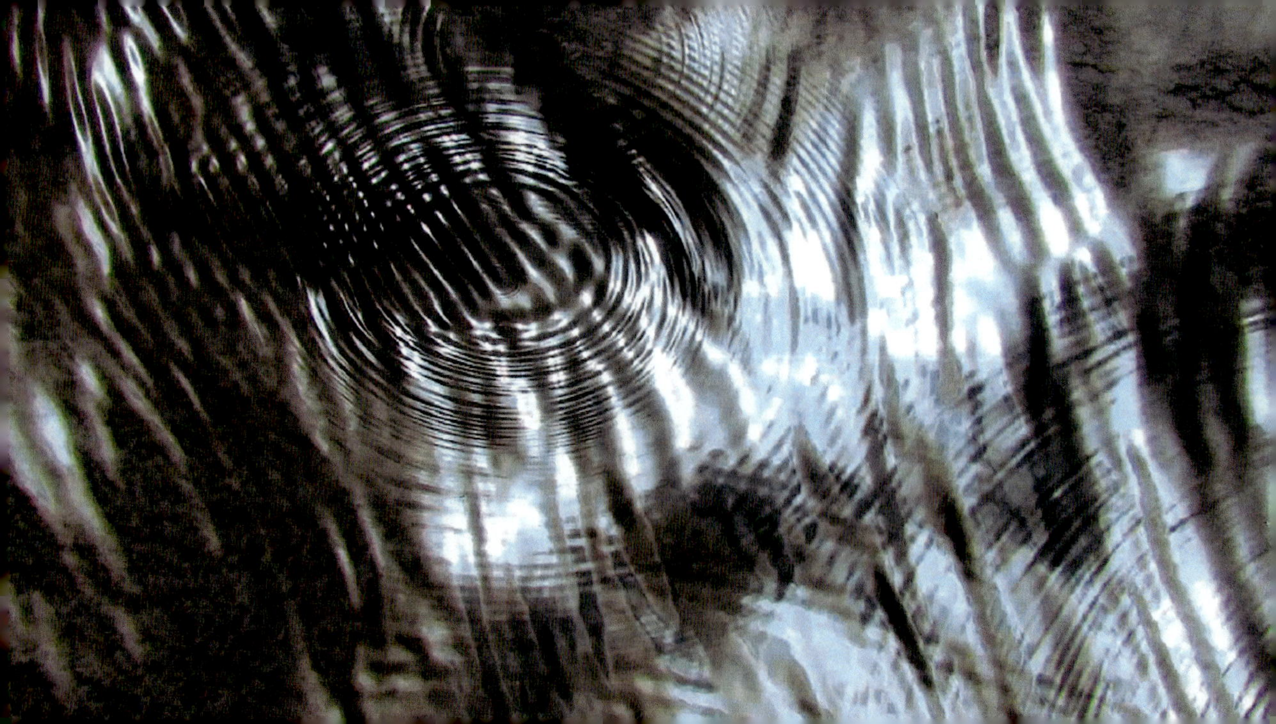

Geyser

One:
What is life, but a line written in water?
Why are we drawn to each delicate manifestation
only to see its dissolution?
Why does each cup of light hold also a drop of black
that grows with each passing day;
poisoning us as we drink?

Two:
Or is each shimmering sculpture the whole of God?
Is each dissolution a revelation,
and the ache of loss only the pain
of smallness we believe ourselves to be?
What's the lesson of the curious cat's paw
that touches my chin like the landing of clouds?

Three:
I keep defining borders, naming names,
but love ever escapes these traps.
Looking into those deep black wells I call eyes,
which the cat calls by no name,
only silence is needed to exchange essence.
The delicate incessant transience,
and the piercing clarity of eye, or leaf edge, or wake of water,
mingle, spread, leave, dissolve, become.

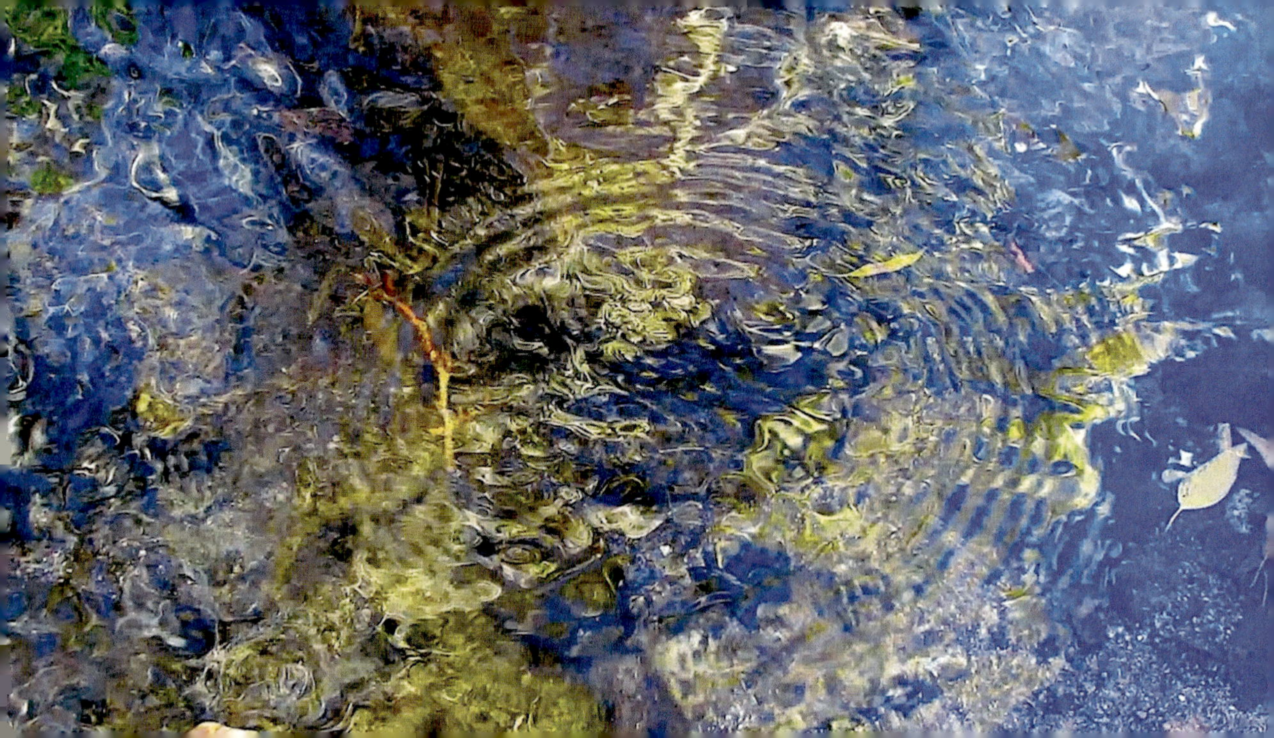

Karma

I,
like a drop into the world,
fell,
compounding the sin of being
by feeling
one,
apart and alone.

I,
like a cry to God,
rose,
compounding the sin of being
by desiring
more,
apart and alone.

The drop and cry fell and rose
in perfect measure from their source,
and the true story to tell is in their meeting.

By the waters of this pool,
joining and dissolving,
reflecting and absorbing,
Here now,
at the center of the ripple,
listen,
Drink.

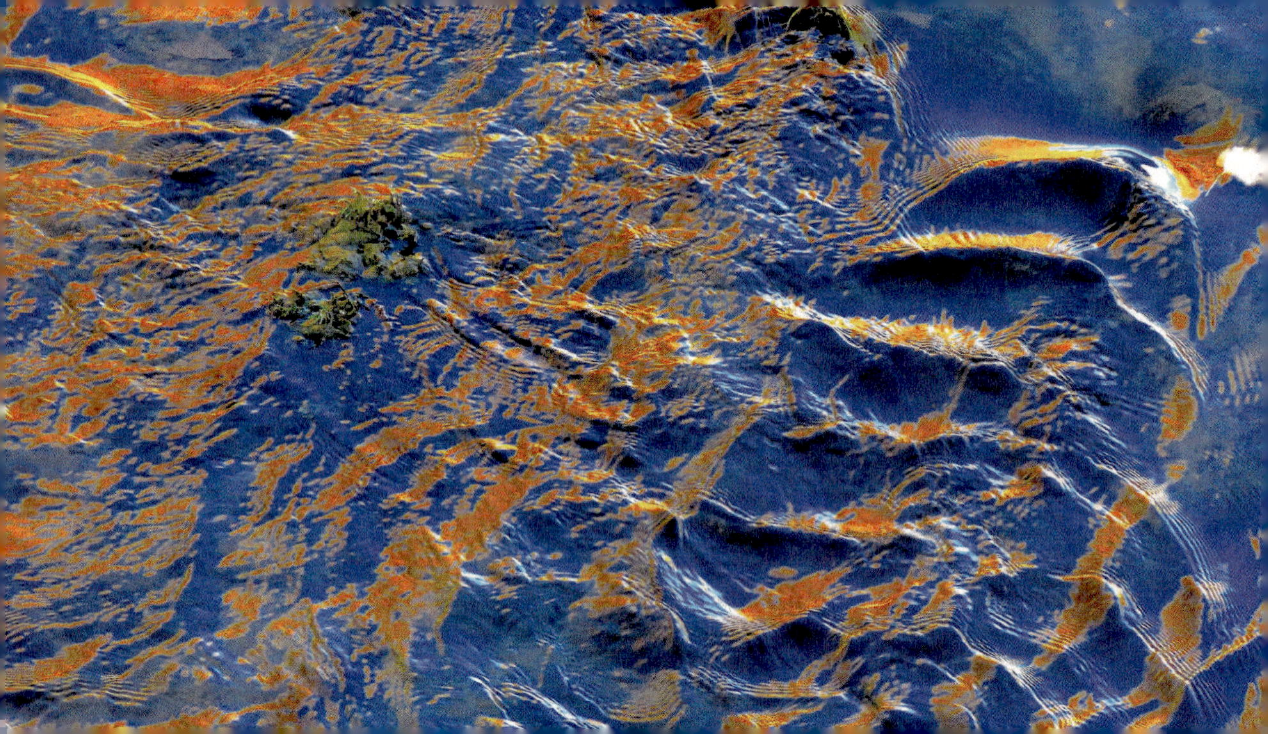

Wave Lines

Clouds curtain open
and waters dance
with mirrored light
advancing and retreating
across time.
All manner of life and death
flows with this river,
yet the sound remains the same—
an eternal, immutable pause
between....

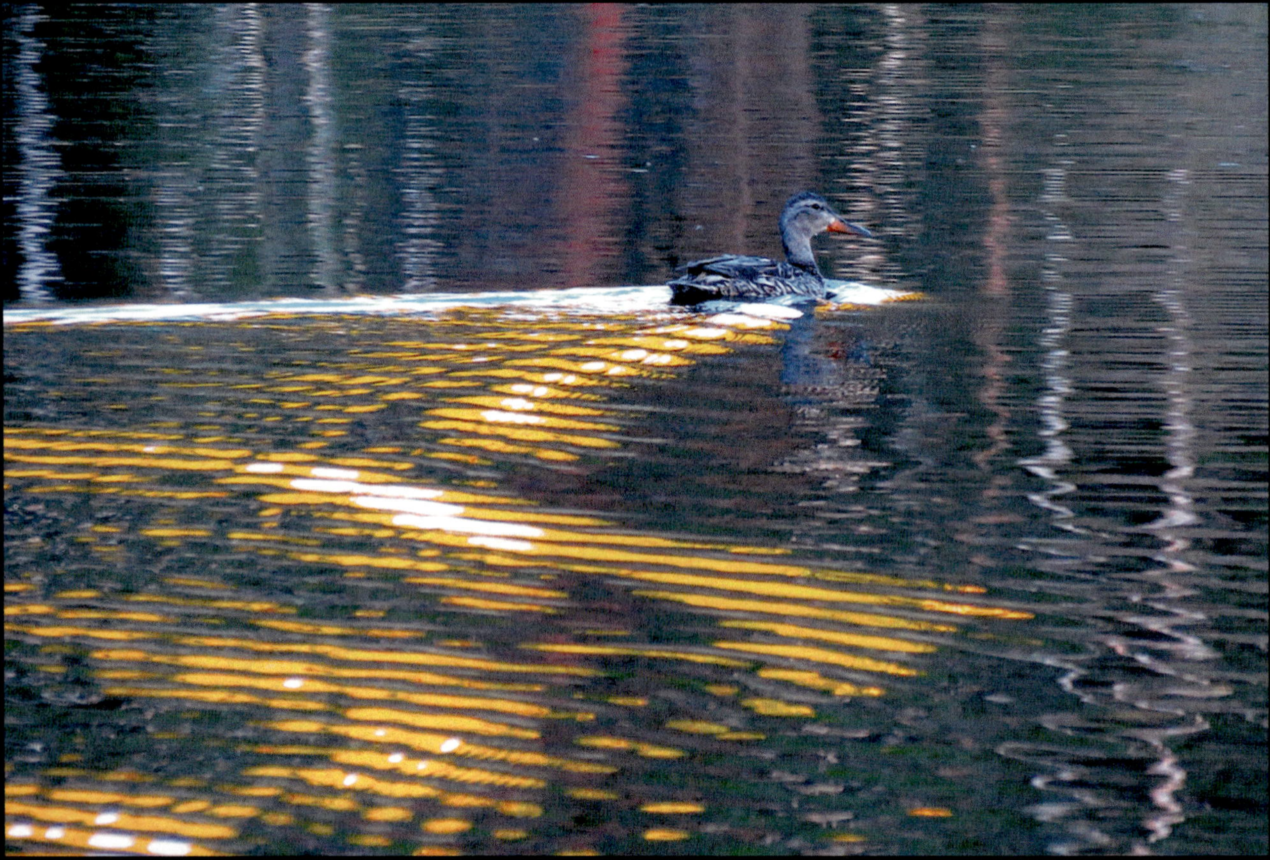

Duck Draws

Will you dare stand with me
by the water?
And leave your earthy dreams
for a mystery that ever waits?
A voice spoke upon the face of the waters
and all was born in its wake.
Your reflection floats upon that same water.
Under the water and behind your eyes
is a singular place of being.

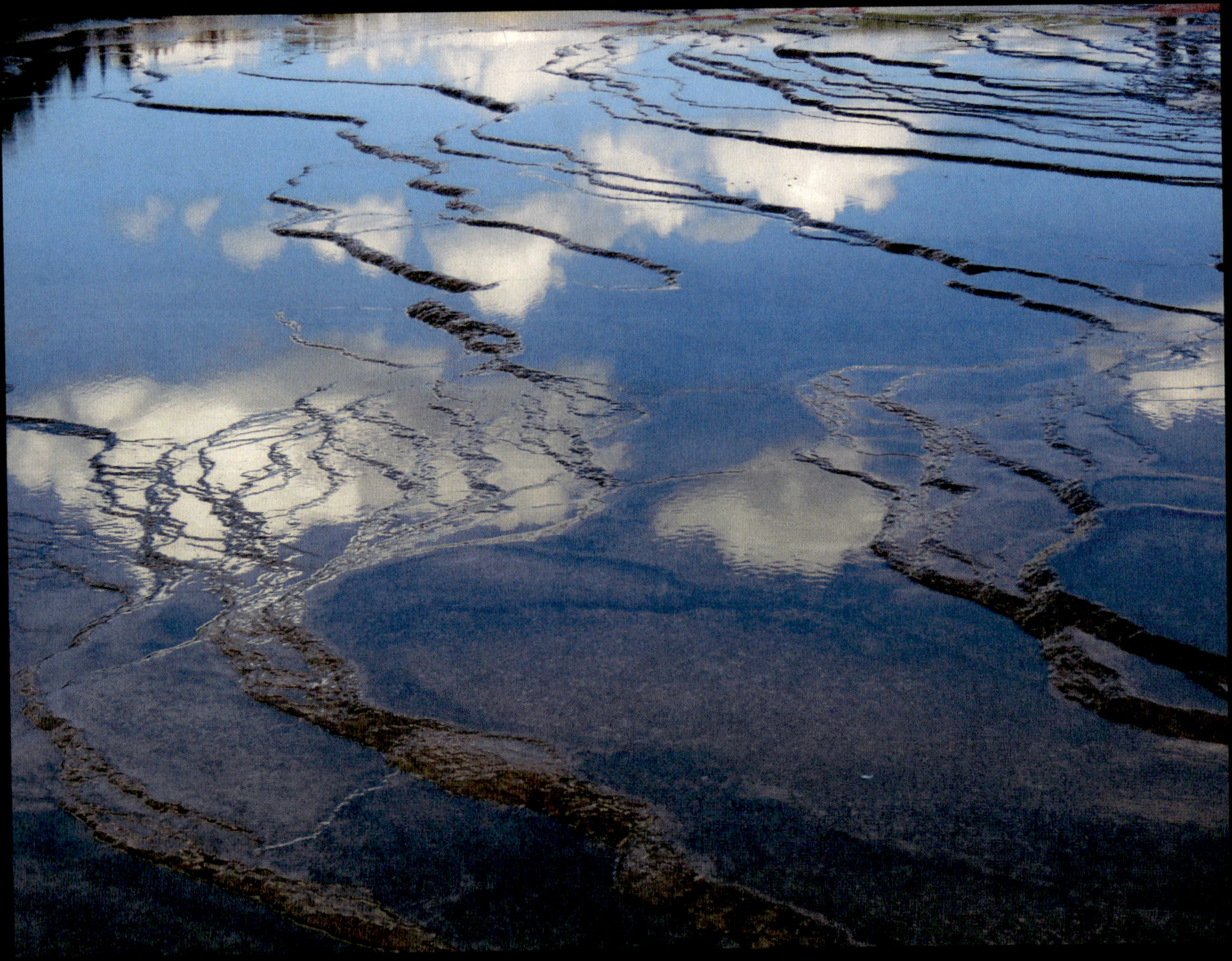

When Is Blue Sky Enough?

I'm traveling, unraveling ambition to be
anyplace other than here.
My sky must be oceanic
and love titanic—as deep
as the eye of God who watches over me.
My sky must mean, must be
indigo, azure, sapphire, cobalt;
must serve my canvas of shades.

I can't stop, can't even ask,
"When is blue sky enough?"
Blue.
Only blue.

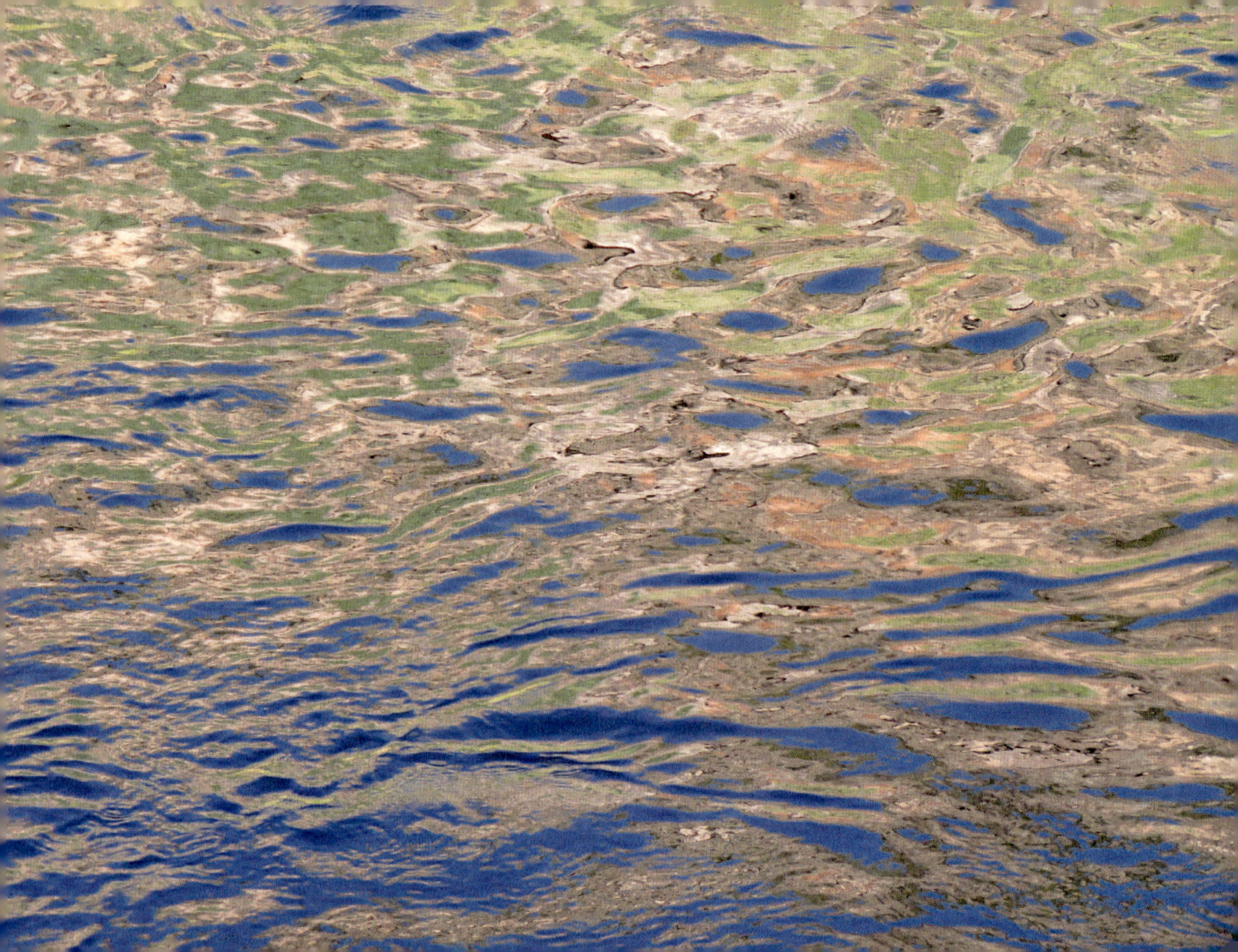

Water Colors

Would you go back for just one night?
Brush your hand along the form of love,
stand in awe of the smell of a small room,
sweep up all the sounds of living
and fill your mind with a moment forever.

Would you go back for just one night?
Ease into your memories,
resurrect the embers,
and dance with flame shadows.

Would you go back to what seemed to be,
to what was only in memory?
Would you go back,
would you stay,
would you go forward,
would you do anything rather than notice today?

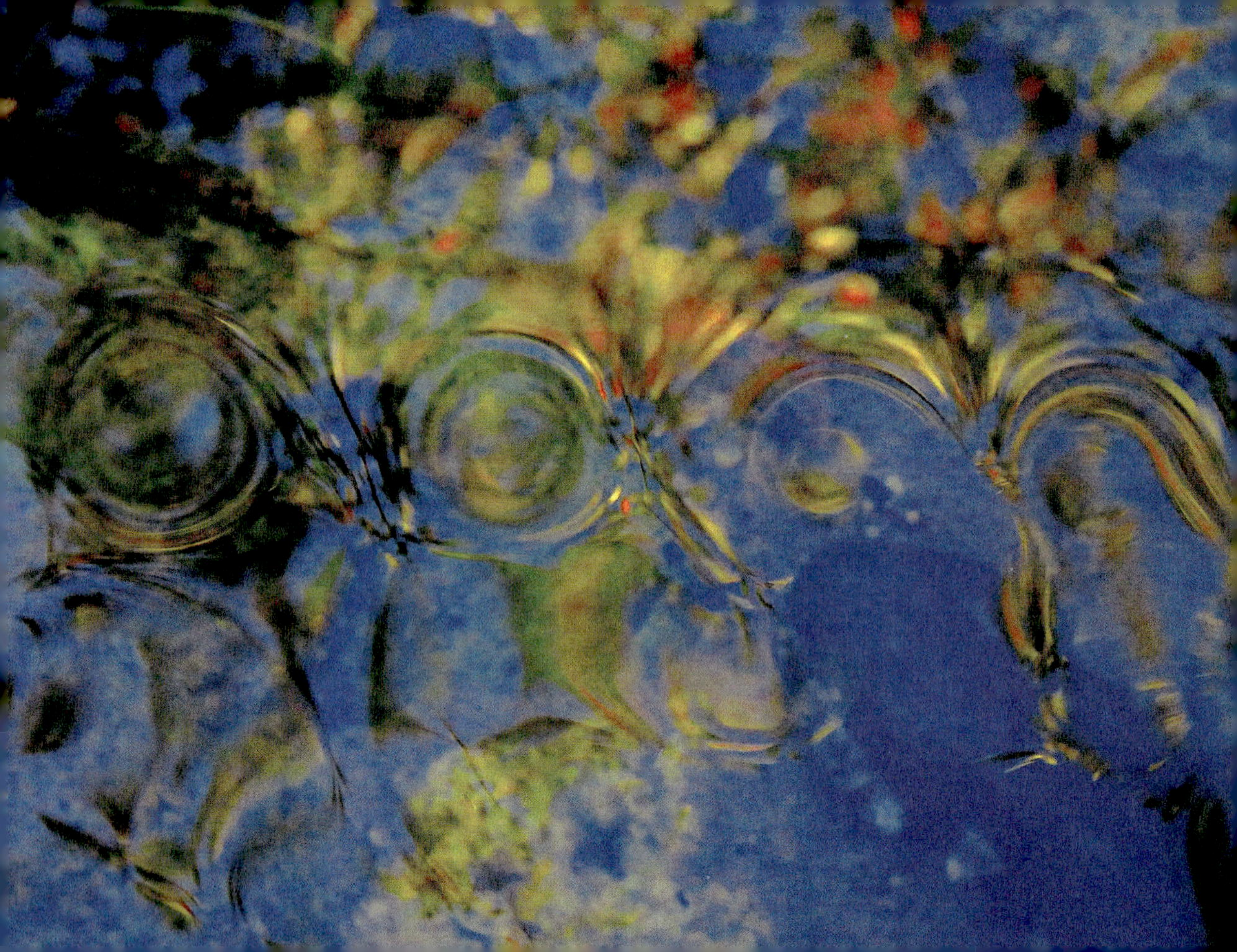

Grace

I have nowhere to be.
No later.
No center.
A pool without wind or tides,
Without a mischievous child with stone in hand.

I have nowhere to be.
Lover.
Loser.
Loudspeaker.
Holder.

I have nowhere to be.
Centered.
Whole.
No launch point.
No linchpin.
Only mystery.

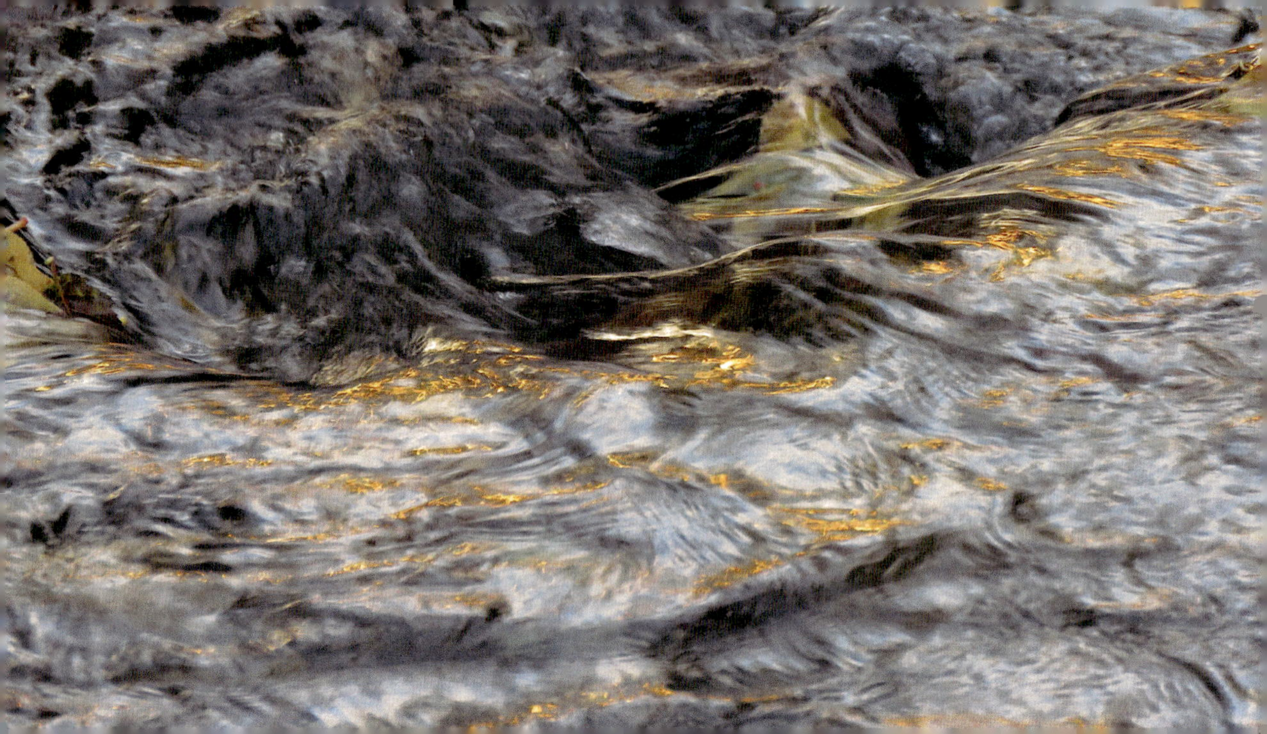

Sunset On Rio Hondo

Stop your frantic motion.
There is nothing that must be done.
In stopping, there is nothing to be;
nothing to hold.
Around the corner from action,
is perfect emptiness.
The fields of motion, of time, and of life
are all the same.
Your voice is heard by no one.
No word was ever spoken.
These words—your words—silence ....

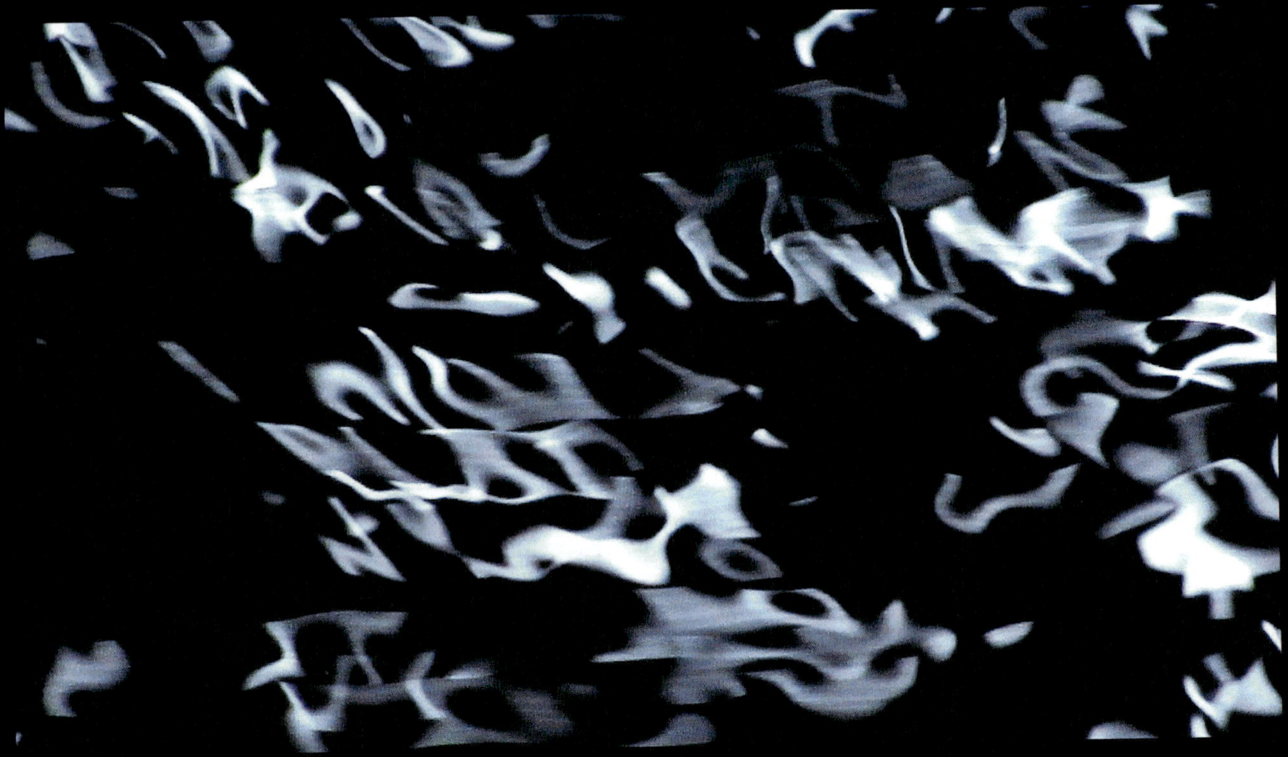

Moon Glyphs

Beyond rightness,
what is Reality?
The mind grasps perfection,
but what is an Eternity?
Beyond the balance of life and death,
beyond the mind, bursting thought:
"Nothing to cling to or stay your fall."

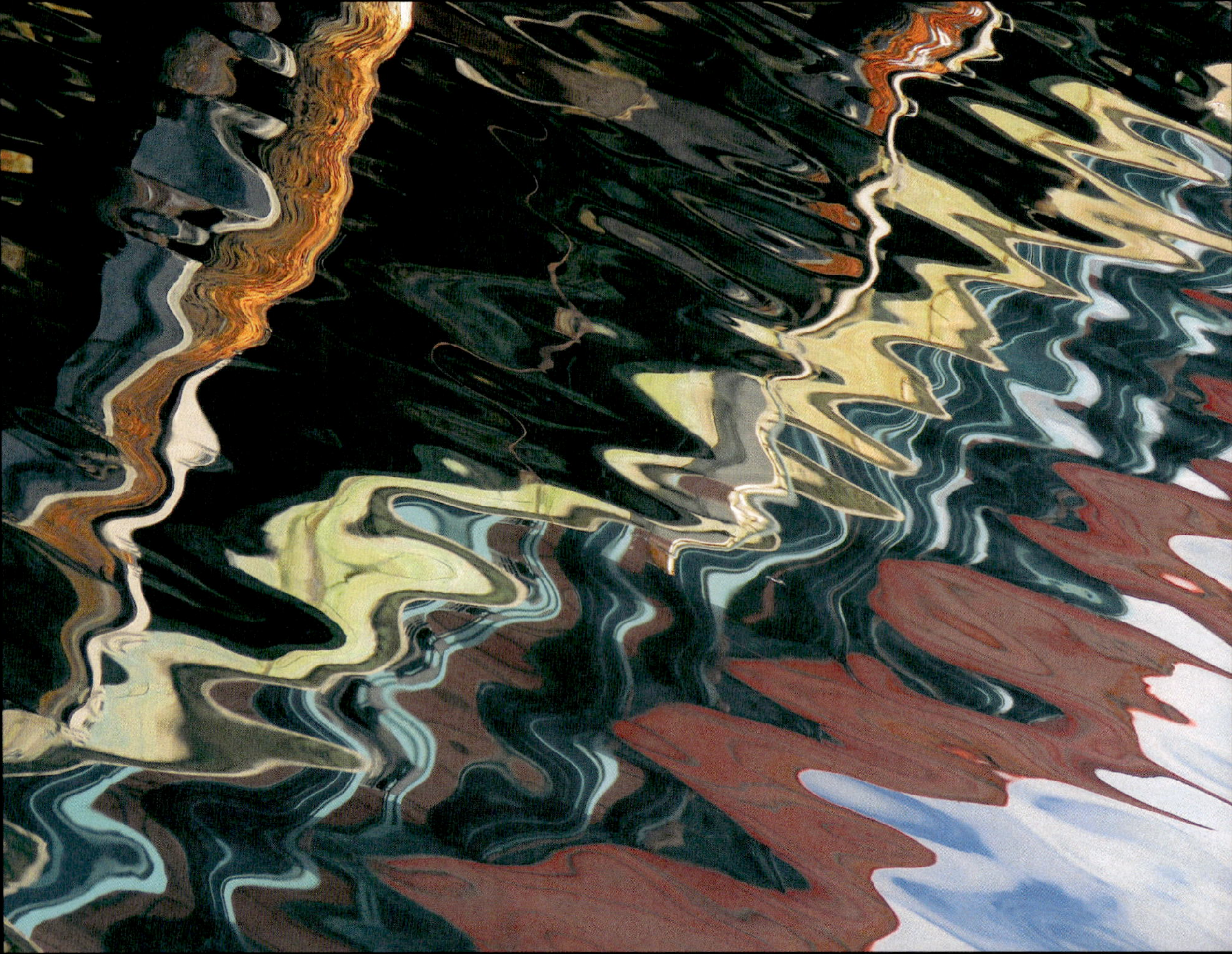

Under The Dock

The river holds me spellbound.
A crow's call echoes off that mirror surface
and down my eyes.
Was love likewise an echo?
And fear,
and hope,
and hunger?
What surface is deep inside?
Over what does life echo?

These words tumble above a still expanse.
I see it now.

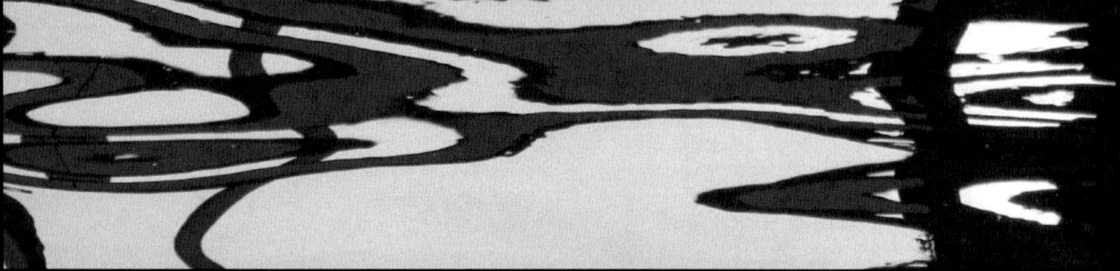

Dock Reflections

Moon shadows on a cloudless night
burn brightly.
Their stark edges reflect where I stand:
inside and outside, poised between this and that.
It's cold, but I don't want to move.

Instead, become quiet;
soak up what it means to be hollow.

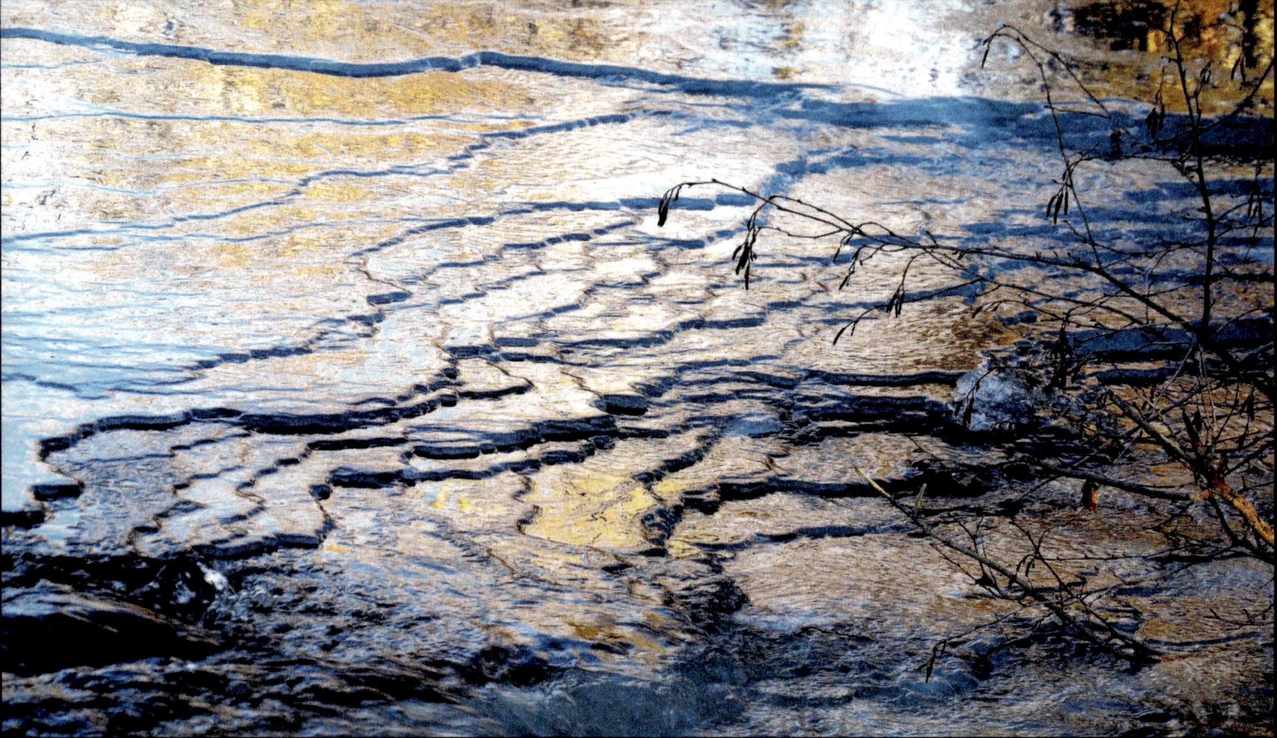

Frozen Hondo

Seeing:
A stem holding tight to its directive,
bending against elemental imperative,
bobbing, then releasing millennia of scheming
to the Fates in a breeze that situates
mysteries

Feeling:
Within the infinitesimal slice of time
this pen tip dragging from left to right to rhyme
across paper,
significance waning,
magnificence draining,
and the gleaming gesture of the miracle of molecules
arcing from river to sky and back again,
tumbling through the page, and the age,
and the wailing

Saying:
The clear line of this message directed,
becoming these words selected.
We are Earth walking.
Our veins the water rippling.
Our limbs the ocean drifting.
Our minds the mist lifting.
Our skin the flower gifting.
Our hearts the dove nesting.
Our souls the Hondo vesting.

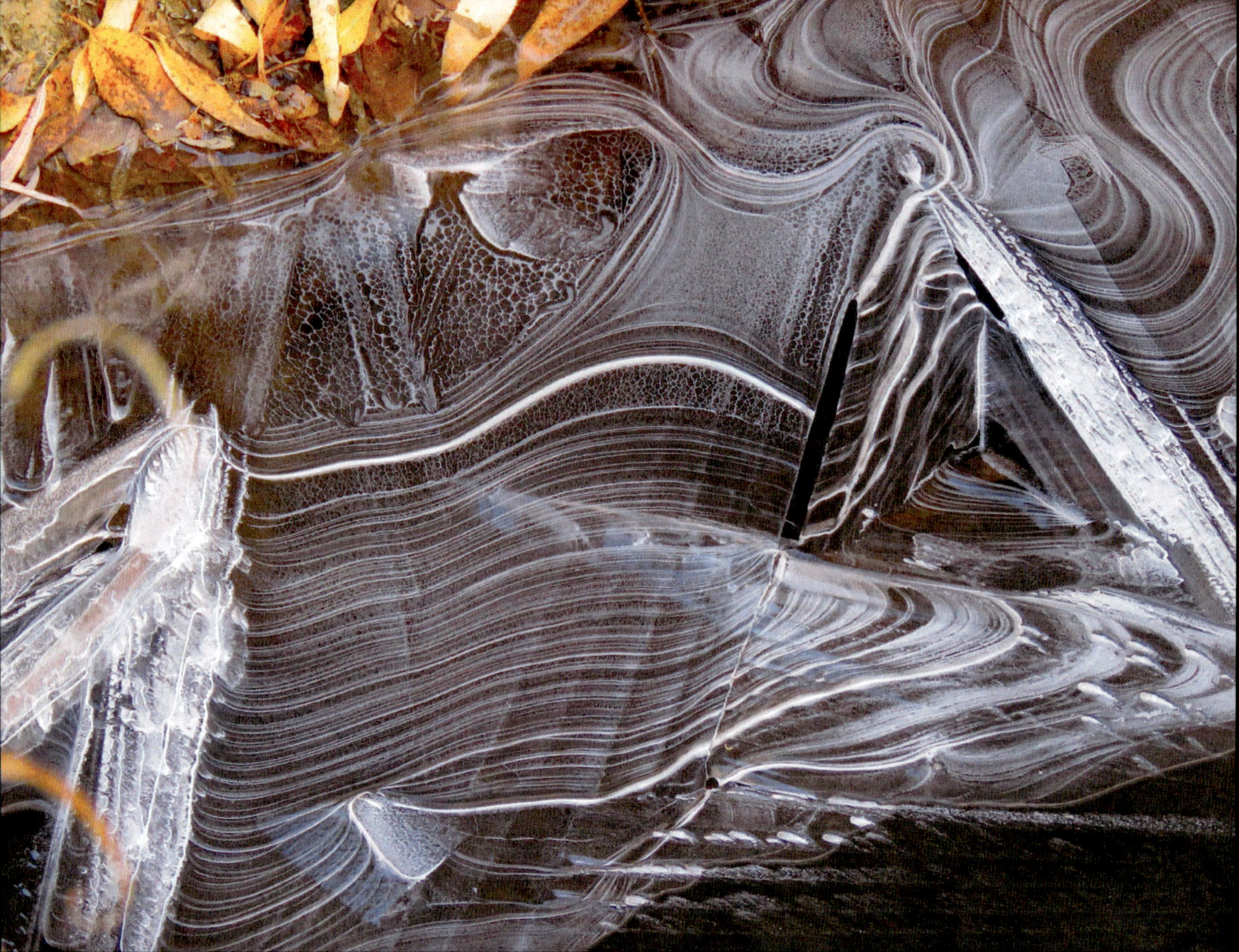

Today

Sit with me
without touching,
without grasping,
without holding.
Restraint waivers
as you reach for words
that are too cold,
too coarse
to contain anything but yesterday.

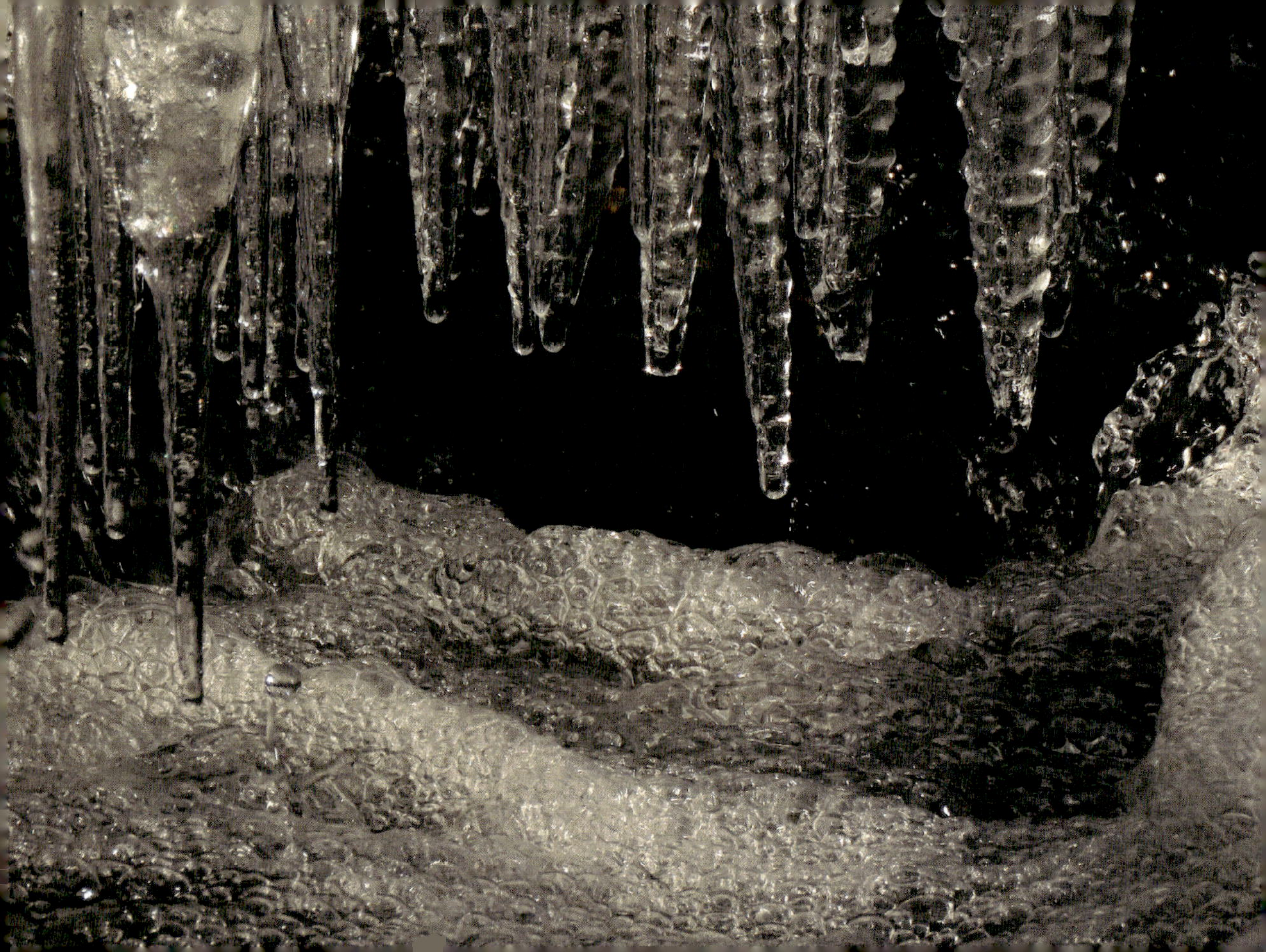

Icicle Factory

I am the love of emptiness
for that which fills it.
Not a love of need,
but simply of existence.
All things are within my grasp
and I hold to none.
Even I am within my Self,
as I who write am startled
by the witnessing, and the witness
is startled by the Darkness
that exhales it.
Darkness am I—
dark to the human eye.

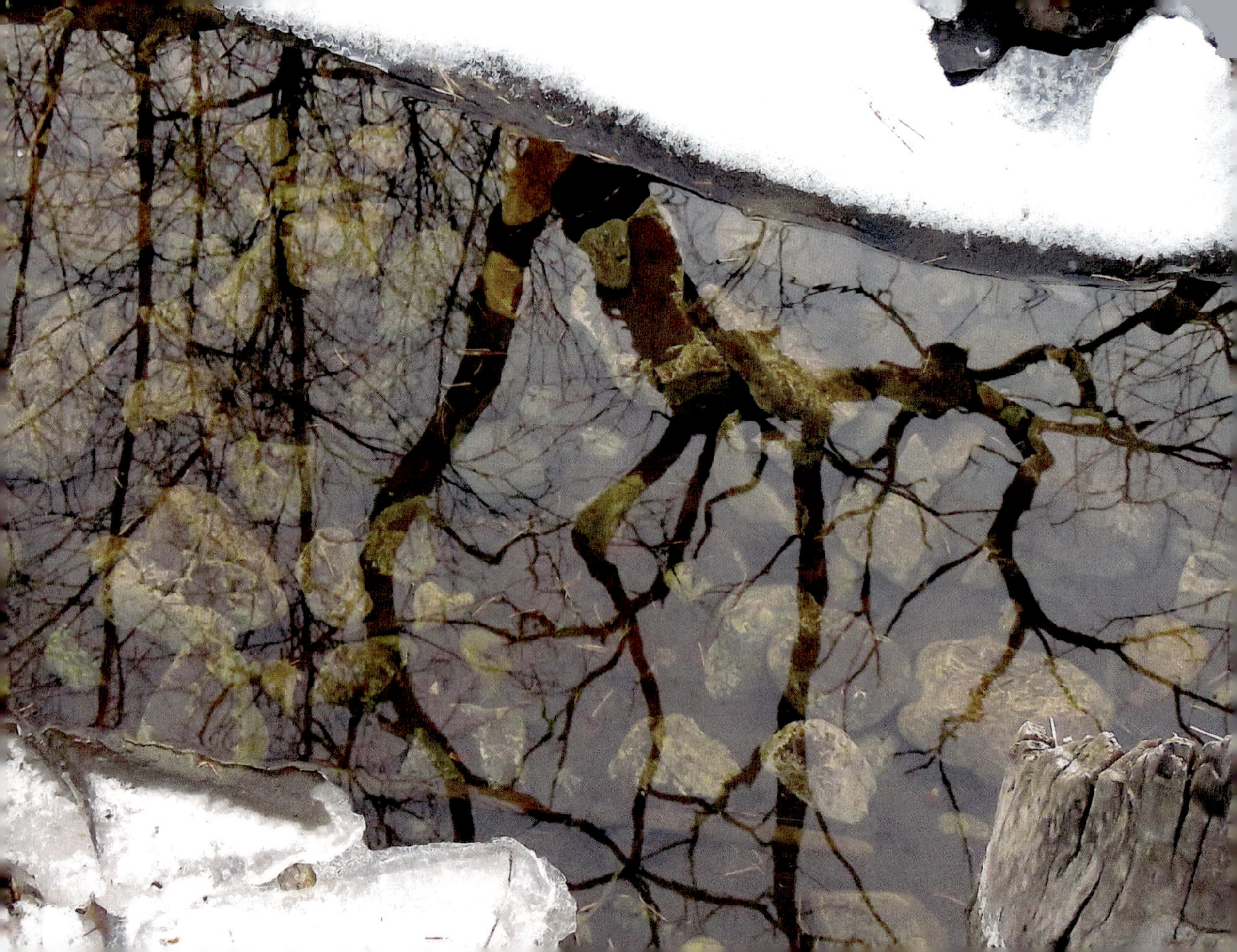

Rock Bottom

It's November
and the whole sordid, gorgeous,
convoluted and crazed mess of a year
comes dribbling out of the trees
till there's nothing left but bare existence:
the skeletal sense of being
branches and roots of hope
tied to this earth.

"I Am" is a lone tree on a weathered hill,
a forest overflowing the valley,
rot and cambium,
the ant's long path and short life,
stomata, stem, and spring.

For you,
so used to finding satisfaction in temporary answers,
Here,
I leave you with none.

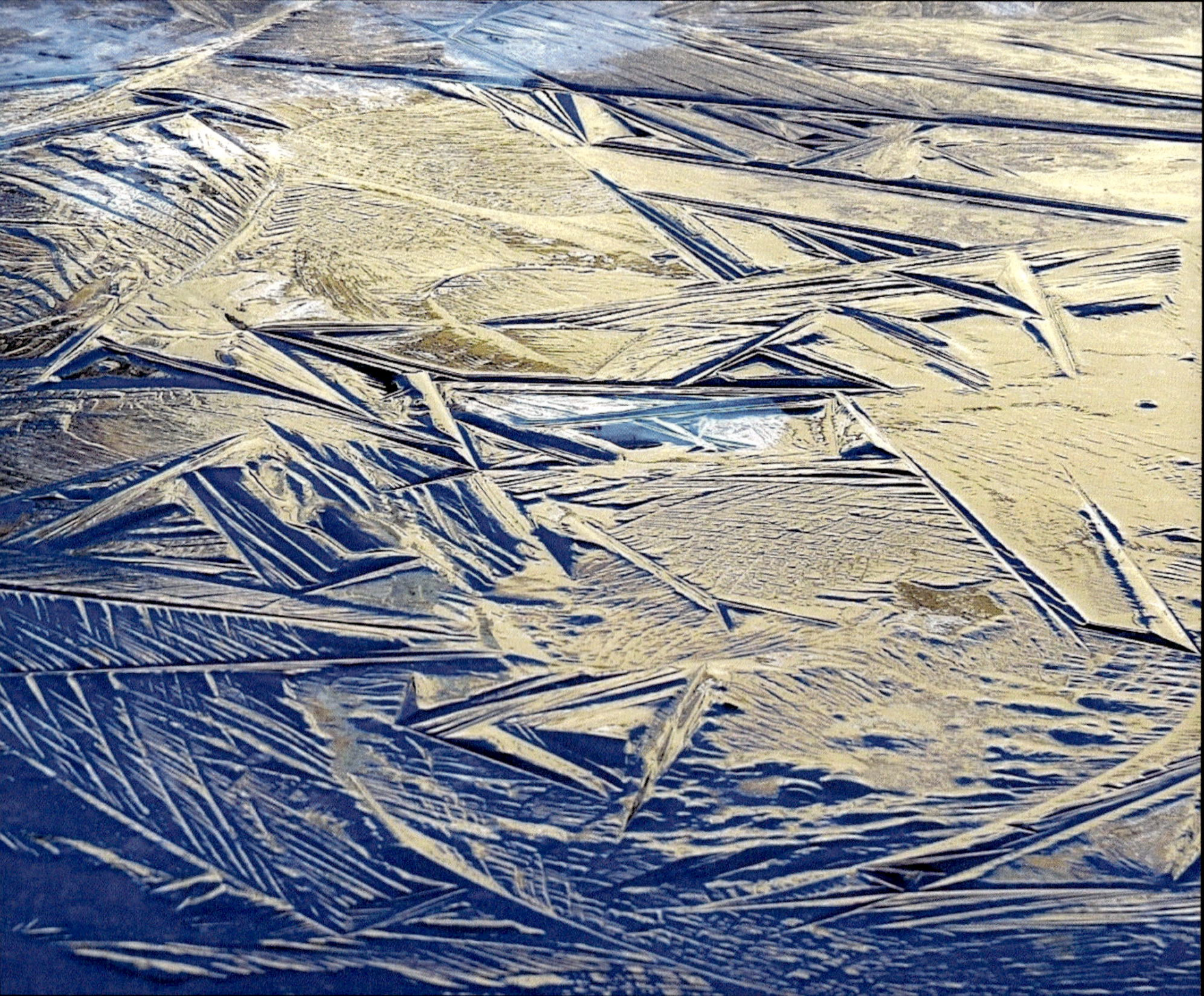

Geometry Of Ice

My words are your words—
our words are God's words.
Words written on a screen of empty space.
Words of a night so still
that all of our self is lost in silence.
A silence you carry with you,
in the heat of action,
and in the depth of sleep.

I will clasp your hand
which is not your hand, nor mine.
For we are alone.
The eye looks upon itself, looks upon emptiness,
and freezes in a view without a viewer.

Alone.... Taste the word.
Speak it on the empty plain that is your life.
The fields of drama are yours alone—
even you shall not remember them.
I will haunt you to your last days.
I who am you.
That which is Real.

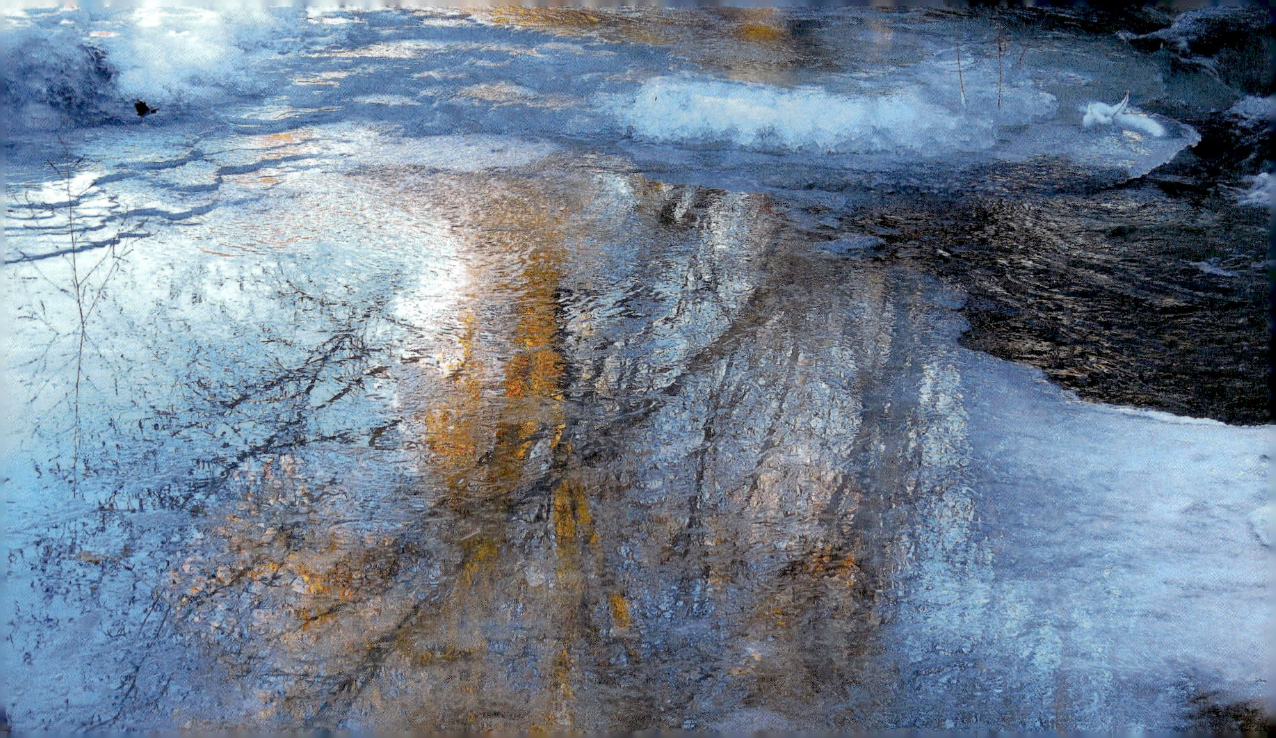

ICE SKETCHES

The world moves:
jays crisscross the sky,
clouds stretch across a blue expanse,
roosters call across the hills
and rise to the challenge of life.
An old hound bellows,
reminding himself of his self,
and the grass sways in tune with sing-song warblers.

Yet every sound slides across solid ice,
every response is a reflection in glass,
and our soul,
the soul,
is infinitely wide and deep,
smooth and still.

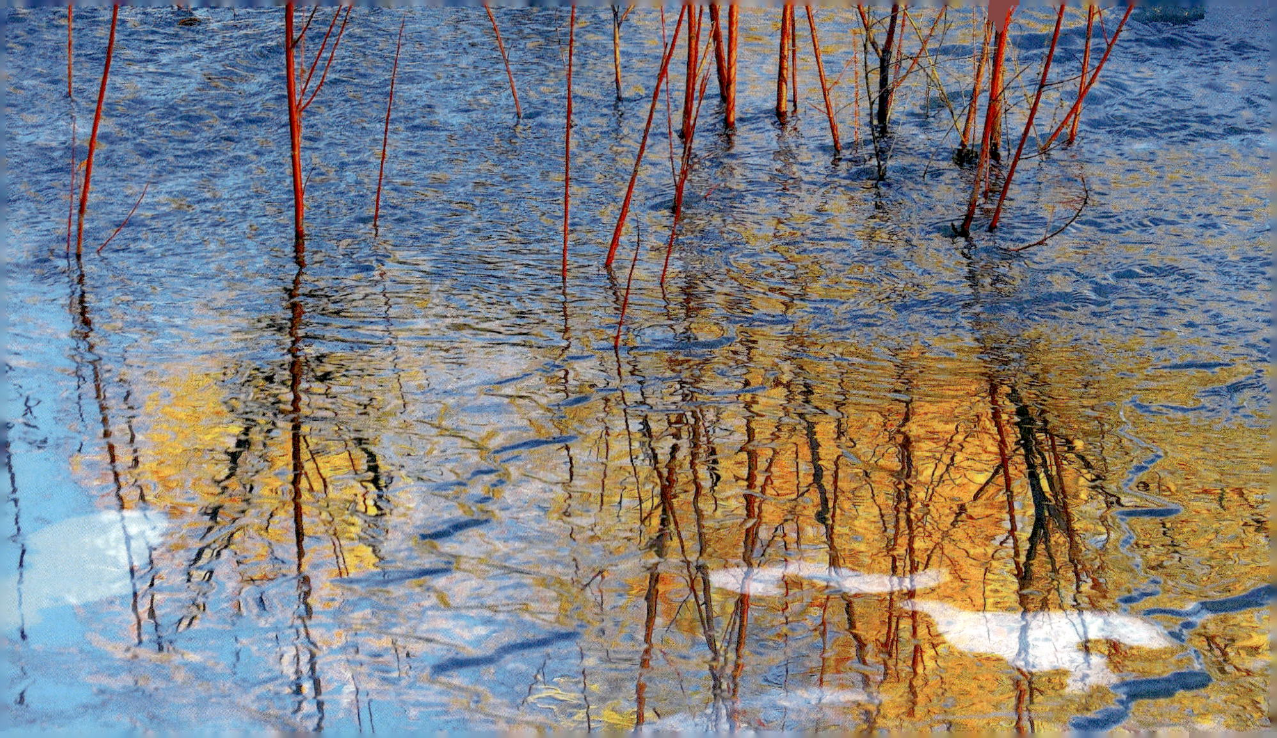

Where Once I Was Empty, Now I Am Full

Words flutter from my mind on a dying breeze.
Now is the awkward silence of true farewell,
The moment before turning your back
On all you hoped would be.

Turn away my love.
I was with you from the beginning.
I was always behind you
And in front.
Yet you will only see me in the full light
Of the turning
Between this and that.

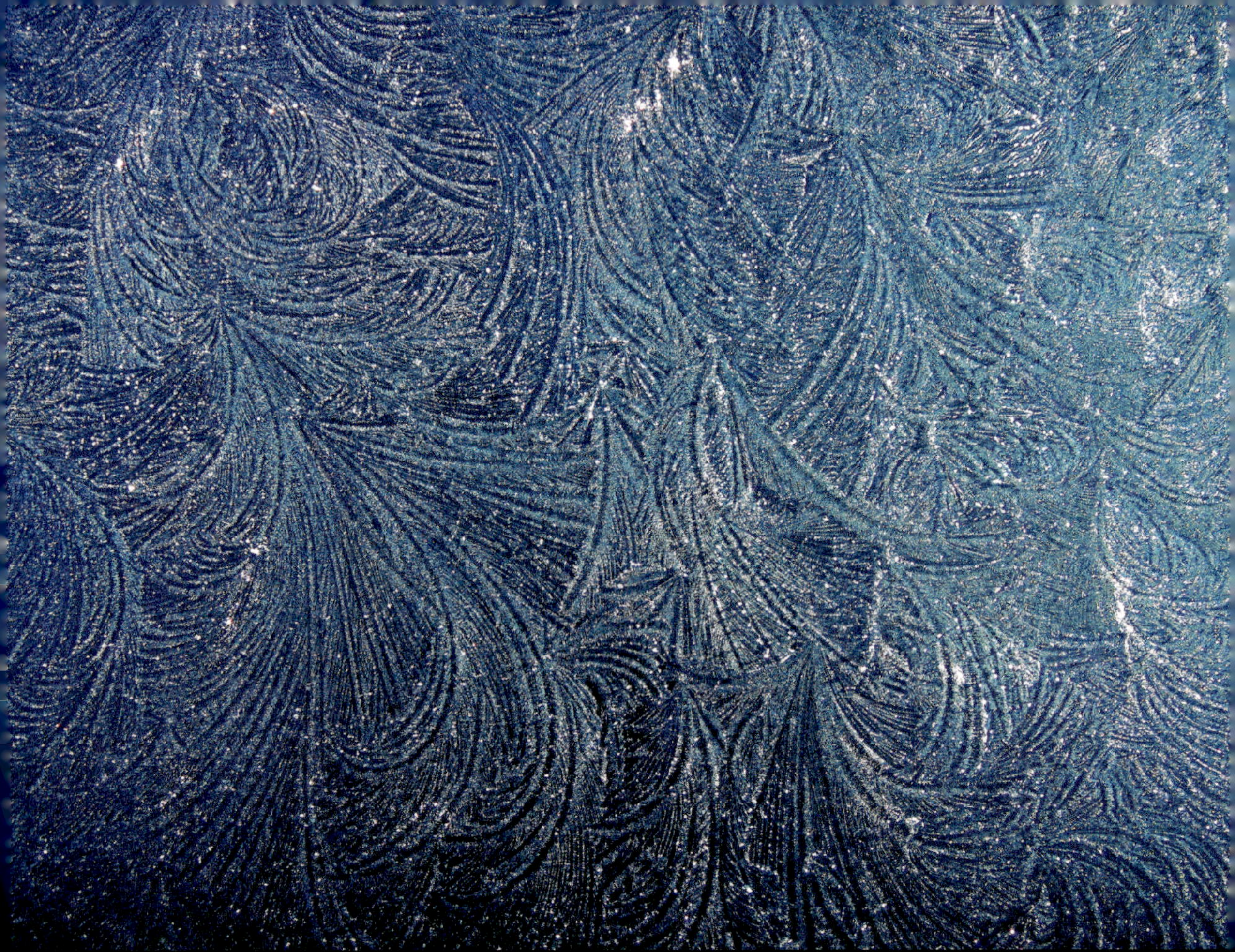

Happy Artist

Expectation requests a location,
a center among these swoops and swirls,
but the more I seek an edge or angle,
the more the self begins to dangle
and truth untangle
the anchors of this scheming,
the suggestions of dreaming,
and figments of meaning.

Between the losing and the loving,
between the beat and the rest,
the heart is a clear glass chest
opening at sun's set
releasing its warmth, yet
in deepest night sky met, measured, and set.

Here, our flourishes find frozen rest,
the print of our heart's love manifest
by the happy artist behind us all
fixed in the gravity of a nameless Call.

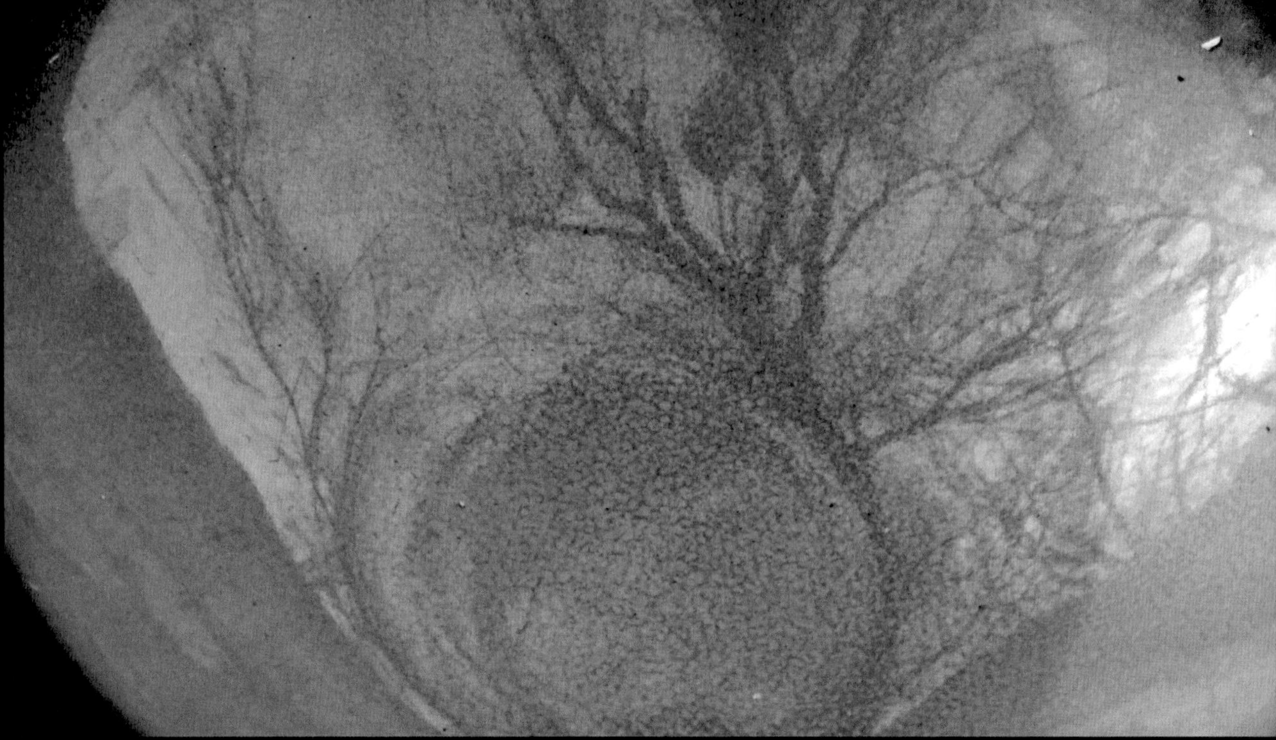

VEINS

O' watcher,
in all your forms
I see you.
Each ripple rests within its motion,
waiting between moments,
ever malleable,
ever content,
ever still.
Still as the space between the blade and the cut.
Still as the pause between the word and the sound.
Still as the edge between form and space.
You are the water of my soul.
You are with me always.

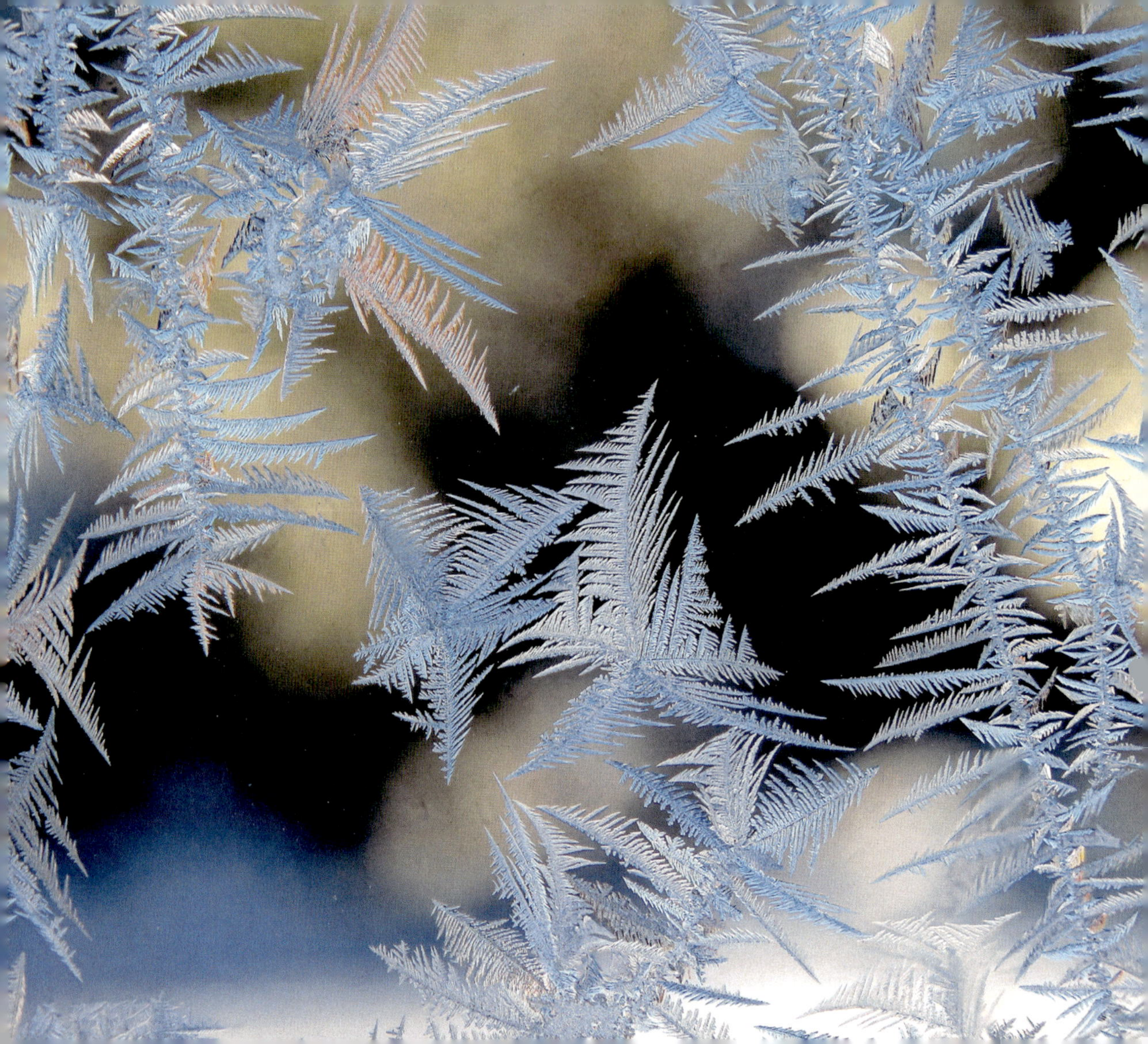

Frost Revelation

The end begins like this:
The self, etched like a delicate line of frost
across a clear and deep expanse,
pauses by the power of will,
and is held by grace until
a tinkling bell of light, robed in clearest white,
melts all thought in sight.
What seemed a sense of lack,
a darkness so compact,
reveals a Golden Find at last.
Yet, what is the source of *that*? He asks.

The mind wracks itself to explain,
rises even higher to remain,
and finds a Dazzling Dark that contains
all the worlds in its reign.
A blackness on high,
a thundering stillness to the eye,
a world of gods, another land,
holding All in its hand.
Yet, what is the source of *that*? He asks.

The minute unwraps its plenitude,
eternity unfurls its grasp,
and serenity lets go its mask,
while all that ever is or was or will be
succumbs to infinity.
The sense of dreaming drops,
and the rhythm, the everlasting rhythm of being,
stops.

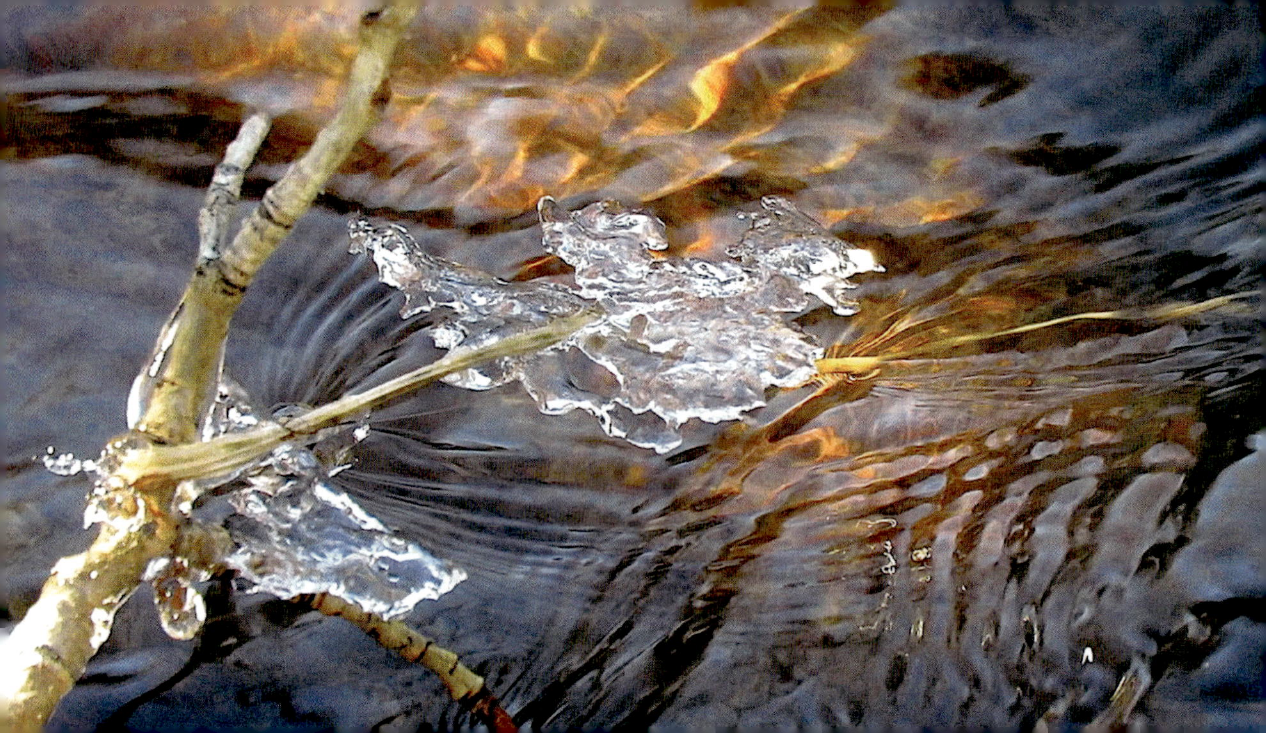

Forks On Fire

The crisp crunch of the path underfoot
gives way to murmuring waters.
Stopped in my tracks, paused,
I've found a way to the edge again.
To the place where self rises,
masked as thought, pronounced into the world,
a form clinging to its hollow core
but melting like a memory,
like ice
above these forks on fire
where left and right dissolve
and a golden flame of silence underlies all.

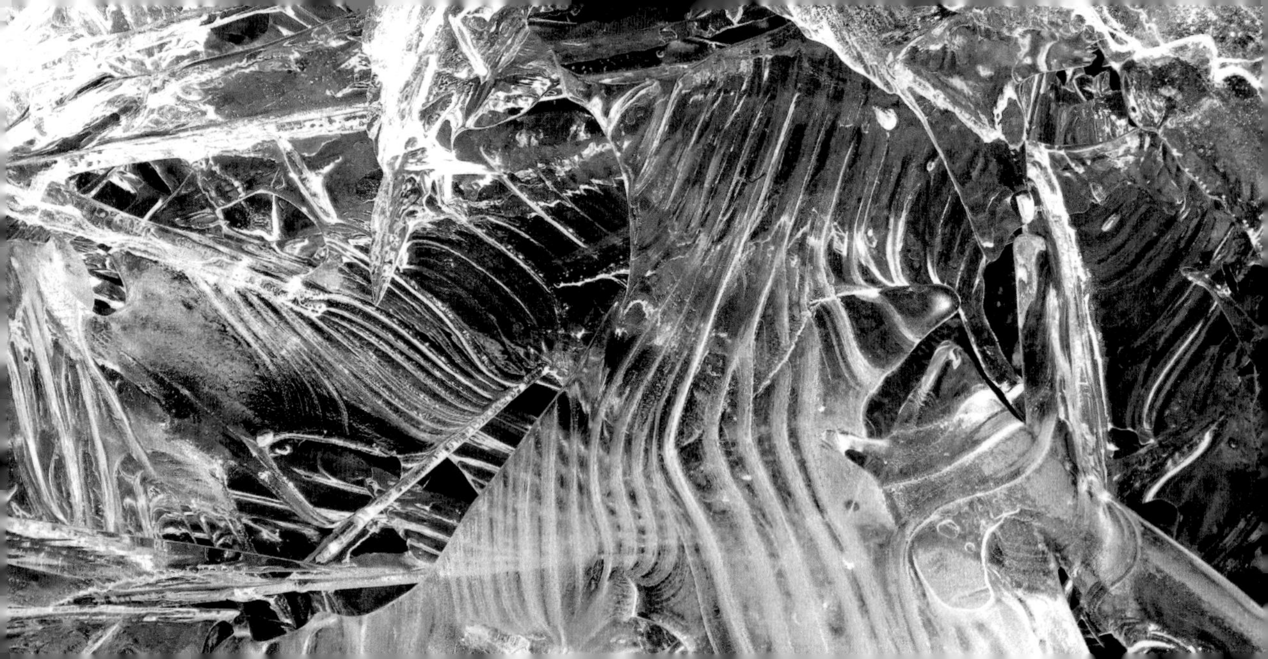

Ice Ribs

Each word we speak in Truth
is a dying.

But you say you want to live

An exposure of our emptiness,
a revelation of the core,
of no control,
and no one at the helm.

As captain of your ship

Only an endless expanse of water,
only empty witnesses –
part and parcel of creation.
Our essence is beautiful,
is still,
is nothing.

So here is your skeleton crew.

I write to you, I speak to you, I am with you.
Close your eyes and look,
for in closing one door we open another.
You hear my voice, see my voice, feel my voice inside you.
Where is this place?
In what faint moment of time have you captured these words?
Who watches within even as words appear?
You always lag the crest of the wave
on fragile legs of memory
carrying all your hope; all your being.
What is the next thought in your mind?

It was unbidden.
Relax and witness thought.
One step above the play of words dwell ye,
yet woe to the one who stops there.
Watch the watcher, be aware of aware.
Aware of the feeling I AM.
We are not any witness-able phenomenon
and we are falling together
within our selves
towards a point of no return.
There is no witness to this.
Only unchanging space without end or being,
formless geometry,
no us; no holding back.

Phaedra Greenwood is a creative writing teacher, freelance writer and videographer. In her long career as a writer/photographer she has received many awards including the Katherine Anne Porter Award and the PEN New Mexico Award. In 1988 she won third prize in the national Nikon "Picture America" photo contest. Fifteen of her photos were selected for permanent exhibit at the Los Alamos Medical Center. Greenwood landed in Taos in 1969 and settled in the valley of Arroyo Hondo where she married and raised a family. For fifty years she has lived a quiet life close to nature. Most of her photos are drawn from observations along the Rio Hondo and the nearby Rio Grande. See pgreenwood478.wordpress.com or "Water is Life" at phaedragreenwood.blogspot.com.

Shawn Nevins is an author, advocate, filmmaker and friend based in California. For Shawn's documentary film work, see PoetryinMotionFilms.com. For his other endeavors, including an extensive collection of interviews and reviews of spiritual teachers, visit SpiritualTeachers.org.

Other Titles from TAT Foundation Press

Falling For Truth: A Spiritual Death And Awakening by Howdie Mickoski
Awake at the Wheel: Norio Kushi's Highway Adventures and the Unmasking of the Phantom Self by Stephen Earle
Subtraction: The Simple Math of Enlightenment by Shawn Nevins
This Above All: A Journey of Self-Discovery by Tess Hughes
A Handyman's Common Sense Guide to Spiritual Seeking by David Weimer
At Home with the Inner Self by Jim Burns
Beyond Mind, Beyond Death
Beyond Relativity by Art Ticknor
The Celibate Seeker by Shawn Nevins
Images of Essence by Bob Fergeson and Shawn Nevins
The Listening Attention by Bob Fergeson
The Perennial Way: New English versions of Yoga Sutras, Dhammapada, Heart Sutra, Ashtavakra Gita, Faith Mind Sutra, and Tao Te Ching by Bart Marshall
Solid Ground of Being by Art Ticknor

For more information on the TAT Foundation visit tatfoundation.org.

Made in the USA
Coppell, TX
01 April 2021

52674151R00067